PRESENTED TO

FROM

DATE

EVERY DAY WITH JESUS

365 Devotions for Kids

Charles F. Stanley

Adapted by Tama Fortner

A Division of Thomas Nelson Publishers

Published in Nashville, Tennessee, by Tommy Nelson. Tommy Nelson is an imprint of Thomas Nelson. Thomas Nelson is a registered trademark of HarperCollins Christian Publishing, Inc.

Tommy Nelson titles may be purchased in bulk for educational, business, fundraising, or sales promotional use. For information, please e-mail SpecialMarkets@ThomasNelson.com.

Unless otherwise noted, Scripture quotations are taken from the International Children's Bible®. Copyright © 1986, 1988, 1999 by Thomas Nelson. Used by permission. All rights reserved.

Scripture quotations marked NCV are taken from the New Century Version®. © 2005 by Thomas Nelson. Used by permission. All rights reserved.

Scripture quotations marked NIV are taken from the Holy Bible, New International Version®, NIV®. Copyright © 1973, 1978, 1984, 2011 by Biblica, Inc.™ Used by permission of Zondervan. All rights reserved worldwide. www.zondervan.com. The "NIV"and "New International Version" are trademarks registered in the United States Patent and Trademark Office by Biblica, Inc.™

Scripture quotations marked NKJV are taken from the New King James Version®. © 1982 by Thomas Nelson. Used by permission. All rights reserved.

Scripture quotations marked NLT are taken from the Holy Bible, New Living Translation. © 1996, 2004, 2007, 2013, 2015 by Tyndale House Foundation. Used by permission of Tyndale House Publishers, Inc., Carol Stream, Illinois 60188. All rights reserved.

ISBN-13: 978-0-7180-9854-4

Printed in Bosnia and Herzegovina by GPS Group
24 25 GPS 6 5 4

JANUARY

JANUARY 1

A GREAT, BIG LOVE

God created human beings in his image.
GENESIS 1:27

Have you ever thought about how much God loves you? You could spend your whole life thinking about it and still never understand how huge God's love for you is.

For starters, God made you *in His own image*! Just think about that: God wanted you to look like Him—maybe not on the outside, but in your heart and soul. Then think about how God created every treasure in the universe, but He says *you're* worth more than any of them. In fact, you're so special to God that He wants to talk to you and to be part of every single moment of your life. He wants to fill you up with His love so full that when other people look at you, they see His love (Matthew 5:16).

So if you ever wonder what you're worth, remember this: God created you, He loves you, and He says you belong to Him (Isaiah 43:1).

Lord, thank You for loving me with such a great, big love, amen.

**TODAY WITH JESUS . . . THINK ABOUT
HOW MUCH GOD LOVES YOU.**

JUST BECAUSE YOU'RE YOU

God, you are my God. I want to follow you. . . .
Your love is better than life.

PSALM 63:1, 3

Do you ever pretend to be someone you're not and do things you'd rather not do—just so people will like you? Do you ever wish that people knew the *real* you? That they loved you just because you're . . . *you*?

Of course, *lots* of people know and love you. But there's only One who will ever perfectly know and love you, and that's God. He knows everything you've ever thought or done or said, and everything you will ever think or do or say. The good stuff *and* not-so-good stuff. And He still loves you.

When you mess up—when you sin—you might be tempted to think God doesn't love you or want you around anymore. Don't believe that for a second! God *created* you to be with Him, and He *never* stops wanting you to be with Him. There's nothing you can do or think or say that will ever make Him stop loving you. Not ever.

Father, thank You for knowing me and loving me, amen.

TODAY WITH JESUS . . . REMEMBER GOD LOVES YOU JUST BECAUSE YOU'RE YOU.

JANUARY 3

LET JESUS SET YOU FREE

"If the Son makes you free, then you will be truly free."
JOHN 8:36

Have you ever seen a donkey carry a heavy load on its back? Have you ever noticed the donkey can't get that load *off* its back all by itself? It simply can't reach it. A donkey needs someone else to take away its heavy load.

And so do you. "But I'm not carrying any heavy loads on my back," you say. You're right—your load is inside you. It's your bad feelings, like anger, jealousy, sadness, and pain. Those feelings can get buried deep down inside, where you can't reach them. They get heavier and heavier, dragging you down. You need someone to take away your heavy load. You need Jesus. He's the only One who can do it.

Jesus will set you free from your heavy load. He'll comfort you and help you forgive and be joyful. All you have to do is ask—and Jesus will set you free.

Lord, thank You for sending Jesus to set me free.

TODAY WITH JESUS . . . LET HIM TAKE AWAY YOUR HEAVY LOAD.

JOY—NO MATTER WHAT

"I told you these things so that you can have peace in me. In this world you will have trouble. But be brave! I have defeated the world!"

JOHN 16:33

Do you have joy, no matter what's happening in your life? It's possible to have that kind of joy with Jesus.

That doesn't mean that if you follow Jesus you'll never have another problem. But it does mean that Jesus will always stay right by your side. When you're sad, He'll comfort you. When you're afraid, He'll help you be brave. And when you have troubles—and there will *always* be troubles in this world—Jesus will guide you and help you. He'll even use your troubles to help you trust Him more, and He'll bless you with the joy of simply being with Him.

Jesus will never leave you on your own, not in happy times and especially not in troubled times. So the next time you're going through a tough time, don't give up. Instead, thank Jesus for the help and the joy He's already sending your way (Psalm 126:6).

Lord, I'm so glad You're always right beside me. Thank You for helping me, amen.

TODAY WITH JESUS . . . LOOK FOR HIS JOY, NO MATTER WHAT'S HAPPENING.

TRUST AND BELIEVE

"Don't worry, because I am with you. Don't be afraid, because I am your God. I will make you strong and will help you. I will support you with my right hand that saves you."
ISAIAH 41:10

Some people say they believe in God and trust Him, but their lives are filled with fear, worry, and doubt. That's not how God wants His people to live.

You *can* trust God, and you can believe every one of His promises. God wants only the very best for you. When you follow Him and try to obey His Word, He won't let you miss out on all the very best things He has planned for you (Hebrews 11:6). But remember, what *God* knows is best for you might be different from what *you* think is best for you. Trust God—He knows what your soul needs.

Is there something you're afraid of? Or worried about? Talk to God. Ask Him to take away those worries and fears. Trust Him to help you. And don't forget: God is always good. So if He doesn't give you what you want, it's because He has something even better planned for you.

*Lord, I trust You, and I believe You want
only the very best for me, amen.*

**TODAY WITH JESUS . . . BELIEVE GOD IS
DOING GOOD THINGS FOR YOU.**

WHICH WAY SHOULD I GO?

When a man's steps follow the Lord, God is pleased with his ways.

PSALM 37:23

When you've had to make a choice, did you ever wish God would just shout from heaven and tell you what to do or where to go? God promises to guide you and help you, but sometimes it may not *feel* like He is. Don't worry. God really *is* working in your life, guiding and helping you, even when it doesn't feel like it.

God hears you when you pray. He knows everything that's happening, He knows when you aren't sure what to do, and He knows just what you need. He won't hide His plans from you (Jeremiah 29:11–13)—but He probably won't show them all to you at once, either.

God is teaching you to trust Him. While He won't show you the end of this road you're walking, He will show you the next step to take—and He'll always be right there beside you.

Lord, it's hard sometimes, but I trust You to
show me the next step to take, amen.

TODAY WITH JESUS . . . TRUST HIM TO
SHOW YOU WHICH WAY TO GO.

JANUARY 7

WHAT "HAVING FAITH" MEANS

Without faith no one can please God. Anyone who comes to God must believe that he is real and that he rewards those who truly want to find him.

HEBREWS 11:6

What do you really want? Not stuff, like a bike—but bigger things, like your parents to stop fighting or someone you love to stop being sick. Did you tell God about it? Do you believe He'll help?

Believing God—what some people call *having faith*—doesn't mean you know exactly how things will turn out. Instead, it means knowing who God is: that He's always loving and good. Having faith is believing God means what He says, and He will do what He promises (Isaiah 55:10–11).

"But I've been waiting so long, and God still hasn't fixed my problem," you say. Yes, sometimes God will ask you to wait for His answer (Isaiah 64:4). The important thing is to keep believing while you wait—and trusting that He wants only the best for you. You don't have to beg God to keep His promises, because He always will, in His own perfect way.

God, I do have faith. But please help my faith to be stronger when I have to wait, amen.

TODAY WITH JESUS . . . CHOOSE TO BELIEVE—CHOOSE TO HAVE FAITH.

THE MOST AMAZING GIFT

The Lord has set his throne in heaven.
And his kingdom rules over everything.
PSALM 103:19

You have been given the most amazing gift ever. What is it? It's the gift of knowing God. *You* get to talk to God, the Creator of everything, any time you want. What an *amazing* gift!

God knows you too. And guess what? He knows you even better than you know yourself! He knows your past, present, and future. He knows everything you think and feel. And no matter what you'll face today, God already knows all about it, and He has the very best plan to get you through it.

With His all-powerful hand, God can do anything. With His unlimited knowledge, He'll guide you. And because of His never-failing love, He'll make sure that everything in your life will be used for your good—even the tough things (Romans 8:28).

There's absolutely nothing better in this whole world—this whole universe—than knowing God and being known by Him!

God, help me know You just a little better each day, amen.

TODAY WITH JESUS . . . LEARN SOMETHING ABOUT GOD.

THE DEVIL LOVES TO LIE

We capture every thought and make it give up and obey Christ.
2 CORINTHIANS 10:5

The Devil is your worst enemy, and he loves to lie to you. He likes to whisper things into your thoughts—things like, "You're a loser; it's hopeless, so just give up; God's not going to answer your prayer"; and "God doesn't even want anything to do with you." The Devil knows exactly what to say to make you feel terrible.

But remember this: *the Devil is a liar* (John 8:44). Don't listen to him! Those terrible things he whispers aren't true. Believe what God says instead—He never lies to you.

And what does God say? What's His truth for you? When you trust God, you're a winner (Proverbs 16:3). There's always hope because Jesus is on your side (John 16:33). God not only hears your prayers, He answers every one of them (Matthew 7:7–11). And God loves you so much, He'll *never* let you go (John 10:11, 27–28). Believe God. He always tells the truth.

> *Lord, help me spot the Devil's lies, and*
> *show me Your truth instead, amen.*

**TODAY WITH JESUS . . . TRUST THAT
GOD'S WORD IS ALWAYS TRUE.**

GOD ALREADY KNOWS

*"The Spirit of the Lord is in me. This is because God
chose me to tell the Good News to the poor. God sent
me to tell the prisoners of sin that they are free."*

LUKE 4:18

Are there things about yourself that you're ashamed of: bad choices you've made, past mistakes, or something you've done or said that you wish you hadn't? Some of those things may be so painful that you don't want anyone to know about them—especially not God.

But God already knows. He knows all the very best things about you—and the very worst. He knows your deepest hurts, your biggest fears, and your worst mistakes. And He still loves you so much that He sent Jesus to save you (Romans 5:8).

God wants you with Him, no matter what you've done. He wants to talk with you and spend time with you. He wants to set you free from shame—to heal your hurts and wash away your sins and mistakes. Don't be afraid of what God knows. Tell Him everything. And then let God tell you how much you're loved.

*God, You know everything I've ever done or said or
thought, and You still love me. Thank You, amen.*

**TODAY WITH JESUS . . . REMEMBER HE
LOVES YOU, NO MATTER WHAT.**

GIVE YOUR EVERYTHING TO GOD

"Love the Lord your God with all your heart, soul and strength."
DEUTERONOMY 6:5

It's important to give God every part of your life—at home, at school, with friends, in sports—not just at church. If you don't, you'll end up building a wall between you and God.

For example, maybe you keep God out of your friendships, so you can do things God wouldn't like. Or you keep Him out of school, so you can pretend it doesn't matter if you cheat. Or you keep God out of sports, so you can throw a fit after a bad game. You tell yourself God won't notice your sins, if you don't give Him that part of your life.

But God sees every sin, and those bad choices build up a wall that keeps you apart from Him. You can tear down that wall, though, by giving your *whole* life to Him. You'll still mess up sometimes, but if you tell God about it, He'll always forgive you.

Dear God, help me give every part of my life to You, amen.

**TODAY WITH JESUS . . . INVITE HIM
INTO EVERYTHING YOU DO.**

DECISIONS, DECISIONS

Remember the Lord in everything you do. And he will give you success.

PROVERBS 3:6

When you have a decision to make, how do you decide what to do? Do you make a quick choice, or just do whatever your friends do? Or do you take time to carefully think about which choice would be best?

How you make decisions actually says a lot about you. Do you go with what would be the most fun or the easiest or the safest? Are you willing to risk messing up, failing, or just looking silly? Do you do whatever it takes to protect yourself from any kind of pain or sadness?

No matter how you choose to make your decisions, there's one thing you must always include—a talk with God. Ask Him about all your decisions. Only He knows the perfect choices for you. Ask God to guide you with His perfect wisdom, because He'll never lead you to a wrong decision.

Lord, in everything, please show me
what You want me to do, amen.

TODAY WITH JESUS . . . TRUST GOD TO
HELP YOU MAKE GOOD DECISIONS.

GOD CREATES GOODNESS

*We know that God causes everything to work together for the good of
those who love God and are called according to his purpose for them.*
ROMANS 8:28 NLT

I s there some problem in your life that just won't go away? Maybe
it's huge, or maybe it's small, but it's *always* there. You've prayed
and prayed about it, and you just can't figure out why God won't take
it away. It's okay to wonder why, and it's okay if you don't understand.
The important thing is to keeping trusting God—He has a plan for
you and your problem. You just don't see it yet.

God is ruler over everything—yes, even your struggles (Psalm
103:19). And He promises that He'll use everything in your life
for your good, because you love Him. *Everything.* Even that pesky
problem.

So the next time that problem pops up, talk to God about it. Then
trust Him not only to take care of it—in His own perfect way and
time—but also to somehow bless you through it.

> *Father, I'm not sure what good will come from this
> problem, but I trust You to take care of it, amen.*

**TODAY WITH JESUS . . . LOOK FOR THE GOODNESS
GOD BRINGS OUT OF YOUR TROUBLES.**

LIVING CLOSE TO GOD

At one time all these things were important to me. But now I think those things are worth nothing because of Christ.

PHILIPPIANS 3:7

Jesus came to earth and died on a cross to give you the most beautiful gift—the forgiveness of your sins. He took all the punishment for your sins, so you can look forward to living forever with Him in heaven (Ephesians 2:8–9). Because of Jesus, you can talk to God and He will listen.

God wants to spend time with you, listen to you, and help you. He wants you to grow closer and closer to Him, so you can love Him more and more. But there are things that can keep you from getting closer to God, such as: selfishness, jealousy, anger, and hate. To get closer to God, you have to give up those things.

God wants you to be forgiving, kind, and loving to others (Ephesians 4:32). But most of all, He wants you to be like Him. So when you do as God asks—loving Him and loving others—you'll live closer and closer to Him.

Lord, help me to love You and love others, so that I can get closer to You, amen.

TODAY WITH JESUS . . . PUT OTHERS BEFORE YOURSELF.

WHAT'S BEST FOR YOU

Anyone who trusts in him will never be disappointed.
1 PETER 2:6

Have you ever heard someone say, "Not my will, God, but Your will be done"? Do you understand what that means? It means that you believe God will *always* do what's best for you. And even though you may want Him to answer your prayer in one way, you understand that if He answers it a different way, then His way is much, much better. When you trust God, you'll never be disappointed.

So when you face a problem, and you know how *you* want it to turn out, you have a choice to make. Will you trust God and obey Him, even if you don't like His answer? Or will you try to fix it your own way? Remember: when you trust God, He'll never let you down. He will always do what's best for you—and it will be greater than anything you could ever even ask or imagine!

> *Lord, I trust You to do what's best for me. I know You'll never let me down, amen.*

**TODAY WITH JESUS . . . PRAY THAT
GOD'S WILL BE DONE.**

TIME FOR FAITH

I will lead the blind along a way they never knew. I will guide them along paths they have not known.

ISAIAH 42:16

There will be times when God asks you to step out into the unknown. Maybe that's what He is asking you to do today—to do something you've never done before, or to make a choice you wouldn't choose on your own. Everything is new—even strange—and you're not quite sure how you feel about that. That's the time for faith. Trust God to lead you.

If you knew exactly what to do all the time and could handle everything all by yourself, you wouldn't need faith. You wouldn't need to trust God. You also wouldn't get to experience the amazing love, wisdom, and power of God when He works in your life.

When God asks you to do something—especially something new—He'll use the full power of heaven to make sure you're able to do it. So trust Him, and follow wherever He leads you.

Lord, I will go wherever You send me. Help me always do what You ask, amen.

TODAY WITH JESUS . . . GO WHERE HE SENDS YOU.

YOU CAN'T FIGURE OUT GOD

"Just as the heavens are higher than the earth,
so are my ways higher than your ways."
ISAIAH 55:9

Be ready—because there will be times when God's instructions just don't make sense. But here's something you should know about God: He doesn't expect you to understand Him or His ways of doing things. He only expects you to obey Him, even if His instructions seem strange to you.

Think about it: Why would God ask Abraham to leave his home without telling him where he was going (Genesis 12:1–2)? And why would God promise to give seventy-five-year-old Abraham a son, and then wait *twenty-five years* to do it? That just doesn't make sense!

And that's the point. You aren't supposed to understand God. After all, He's the Creator and ruler of everything. He's huge and all-powerful. Your job is to worship and praise Him. Don't try to figure Him out—it isn't possible. Just trust Him, and let Him show you how awesome and amazing He really is.

Lord, I don't understand all the things You do,
but I do know You're amazing! Amen.

TODAY WITH JESUS . . . THINK ABOUT
HOW AWESOME GOD IS.

WHAT ARE YOU WORTH?

I praise you because you made me in an amazing and wonderful way.
PSALM 139:14

How do you decide what you're worth? Is it by what other people say about you? Or how much money you have, how you look, what you wear, your grades, or how good you are at sports? It's tempting to use those kinds of things to decide how valuable you are. Tempting, but wrong! Those kinds of things are always changing. Sometimes they're not even true! And you've probably noticed that it's much easier to believe the bad stuff than the good stuff.

Remember this: the only One who can truly decide how valuable you are is the One who created you and who sent His Son to die for you—*God*. And because Jesus died for you, you are forever loved (Jeremiah 31:3), accepted (Romans 15:7), able (2 Corinthians 3:5), and victorious (1 Corinthians 15:57). Believe what God says about you, because it's the real truth.

Lord, teach me to see how important and
valuable I am to You, amen.

**TODAY WITH JESUS . . . SEE YOURSELF
THE WAY GOD DOES.**

WHAT TO BELIEVE

Lord, give me life by your love. Your words are true from the start.
PSALM 119:159–160

You read it yesterday, but it's so great, you should read it again today. Because of Jesus, you are forever loved (Jeremiah 31:3), accepted (Romans 15:7), able (2 Corinthians 3:5), and victorious (1 Corinthians 15:57).

But sometimes, that is hard to believe. Troubles, hard times, mistakes you've made, hurt feelings, or cruel words from others can make you feel afraid, worthless, helpless, and just not able to deal with your problems.

But remember, "The human heart is the most deceitful of all things" (Jeremiah 17:9 NLT). That means your feelings can lie to you—because of a mistake you made, what someone says about you, or just from having a bad day. But you can always trust what God's Word says. So repeat these words to yourself over and over again: "Because of Jesus, I am loved, accepted, able, and victorious." *That's* what you should believe!

Jesus, help me to believe the truth of Your words always, amen.

**TODAY WITH JESUS . . . REMEMBER
WHAT GOD SAYS ABOUT YOU.**

YOU CAN'T EARN GOD'S LOVE

The Lord wants to show his mercy to you. He wants to rise and comfort you. . . . And everyone who waits for his help will be happy.

ISAIAH 30:18

Do you feel as if you need to *do* something to get God to love you? That you have to win Him over or impress Him? If so, then you're probably trying to *earn* God's love instead of trusting Him to simply give it to you.

You don't have to obey God to *make* Him love you. That's not what God wants. Yes, you should obey Him—when God shows you what to do, then do it. When He points out a sin, tell Him you're sorry and live how He tells you. But don't do it to earn God's love—do it because *He already loves you*—and because you love Him and want to please Him.

You see, God wants to bless you with His love *even more* than you want to be blessed. Stop trying to earn His love. Just accept it—and love Him right back.

Father, help me understand that I don't have to earn Your love because You always love me, amen.

TODAY WITH JESUS . . . BELIEVE GOD LOVES YOU.

TIME FOR GOD

My soul, wait in silence for God only, for my hope is from Him.
PSALM 62:5 NASB

You take time for school, for friends and family, for fun things you like to do. But do you take time for God? To think about Him, listen to Him, and let Him show you who He wants you to be? You should! Because that's how you get to know God and what He wants for your life. It won't happen in an instant. After all, you didn't get to know your best friend after just one visit. To know God, spend time with Him every day.

When you're not spending time with God, He might use a problem to get your attention. He knows if you're worried or upset, you'll turn to Him. And when you do, He'll not only help with that problem, but He'll also fill your life with His love, joy, and peace. You were *created* to be with God—so take quiet time every day to do just that.

*God, I want to know You better. Help me
take time for You each day, amen.*

TODAY WITH JESUS . . . SPEND TIME WITH GOD.

WHEN SOMEONE LETS YOU DOWN

Suppose someone sees his brother in Christ sinning . . .
That person should pray for his brother who is sinning.

1 JOHN 5:16 NLT

When you see someone doing something wrong, it can be hard to understand why they're doing it. But when you see a Christian doing wrong, it's even harder—especially if it's someone you know or look up to. It can leave you feeling confused, hurt, and sad. So what should you do?

First, keep doing what you know is right. Don't allow that person to pull you away from God. And believe God's promise that He'll never let you down—even if others do. Second, pray for that person to obey and come back to Jesus. If he or she has hurt your feelings, forgive. Third, let God comfort you. He'll always be your greatest encourager. Let Him lift up your spirit and bring something good out of this hard time.

Always pray for the one who let you down, but then trust Jesus to take care of everything else. Remember Jesus loves that person even more than you do.

Lord, I pray for _____. Help him/
her to come back to You, amen.

TODAY WITH JESUS . . . PRAY FOR
THOSE WHO DO WRONG.

SIT QUIETLY WITH HIM

"I wish my people would listen to me. . . . I would fill you with honey from the rocks."
PSALM 81:13, 16

God doesn't want to be some faraway God. He wants you to know Him *personally*. Even now He's pulling you closer to Him. He wants you to feel—deep down in your soul—how great His love for you is. And He has things He wants to show you—amazing things that He'll teach you when you're still and quiet with Him.

Sometimes you pray because of all the things that are worrying you, and that's a good thing to do. But the very *best* thing to do is simply to sit quietly with God as you read His Word. Because it's during these still, quiet times that God will give you glimpses of just how amazing He really is.

Don't miss out on the wonders of knowing God. There's no greater joy and no better way to spend your time than sitting quietly with Him.

Lord, I want to know You. Please use Your Word to show me who You are, amen.

TODAY WITH JESUS . . . SIT QUIETLY WITH HIS WORD.

YOU CHOOSE

"The wise man built his house on rock. It rained hard and the water rose. The winds blew and hit that house. But the house did not fall, because the house was built on rock."

MATTHEW 7:24–25

The things you face today can either build you up or tear you down. The good news is that you get to *choose* which it will be. You can either ask God to help with your troubles and use them to make your faith stronger—*or* you can let those problems knock you down, just like that foolish man's house that was built on the sand. It's your choice.

If you look at your troubles and think only about how *you* can fix them, you'll probably end up getting knocked flat. Turn to God instead. Ask Him what *He* can do with your troubles. Because no matter what you face, God can *definitely* handle it. Go to His Word, read it, and do what it says. God will not only show you what to do—He'll also make you stronger and teach you more about His wonderful ways.

*Lord, help me remember to go to You and
Your Word when I have troubles, amen.*

**TODAY WITH JESUS . . . LET GOD USE YOUR
TROUBLES TO MAKE YOUR STRONGER.**

YOUR ANCHOR

These things encourage us who came to God for safety. They give us strength to hold on to the hope we have been given. We have this hope as an anchor for the soul, sure and strong.
HEBREWS 6:18–19

There will be days when it feels as if God has drifted away—especially when you're extra busy or when everything around you is changing. Maybe a friend is moving, or you're moving because your mom got a new job, or you're just so busy juggling school, friends, and other stuff.

But no matter what kind of craziness or changes are going on, Jesus *never* changes. He's "the same yesterday, today, and forever" (Hebrews 13:8). And His love for you never changes, either; it lasts forever (Jeremiah 31:3). God hasn't drifted away, but perhaps you have.

If God feels far away, it's time to check your heart. Have you been so busy thinking about other things that you've forgotten about Him? Open up His Word, talk to Him, and listen. Just as an anchor keeps a boat from drifting away, God's Word keeps you from drifting away.

Lord, don't let me drift away. Use Your Word to keep me anchored close to You, amen.

WHAT IS GOD LIKE?

The Lord your God is God. He is the faithful God. He will keep his agreement of love for a thousand lifetimes. He does this for people who love him and obey his commands.

DEUTERONOMY 7:9

What do you think God is like? Whether you realize it or not, the way you think about God will decide how you act toward Him.

For example, if you think God is a loving, wise, and wonderful heavenly Father who takes care of you, then you'll love and trust Him. You'll want to tell Him everything, and you'll follow wherever He leads you. But if you think God is a cold, strict, faraway ruler who's just waiting for you to mess up, then you probably won't love and trust Him so much. You may feel like you *have* to pray to Him, but you won't have a close, loving relationship with Him.

That's why you should read God's Word. Ask Him to show you what He's really like—and you'll discover that the One who created you and loves you is more wonderful than you could ever imagine!

God, take away any wrong ideas I have about You and show me who You really are, amen.

TODAY WITH JESUS . . . USE YOUR BIBLE TO LEARN SOMETHING ABOUT GOD.

BELIEVE GOD!

If any of you needs wisdom, you should ask God for it. . . . But
when you ask God, you must believe. Do not doubt God.
JAMES 1:5–6

God has great plans for your life (Jeremiah 29:11). But the question is . . . are you ready for those plans? Are you expecting God to do great things in your life? And when God shows you the next step in His plan, are you willing to take it?

When you ask God to guide you and He answers you, it's so very important that you believe what He tells you (Mark 11:23–24) and that you do what He says (Jeremiah 7:23). If you don't, then what you're really telling God is that you don't trust Him.

So how do you keep your trust strong? Keep thinking about God—who He is, what He can do, and how amazingly *huge* His love for you is. Believe God and trust Him to do what He says, because His plans for you are greater than anything you could ever dream.

Lord, help me believe You and follow
wherever You lead me, amen.

TODAY WITH JESUS . . . BELIEVE GOD
WILL DO WHAT HE SAYS.

YOU'RE NEVER ALONE

Everything that was written in the past was written to teach us, so that we could have hope. That hope comes from the patience and encouragement that the Scriptures give us.

ROMANS 15:4

The devil is a liar. That's a fact. And one of his worst lies is that you have to face your troubles all by yourself. *Don't believe it!* God promises that "He will not leave you or forget you"—not ever (Deuteronomy 31:6). Not for a single second.

What troubles are you struggling with? Something at school, at home, or with a friend? God is willing and able to help you. He knows just what you need, and He won't let you down. Remember, God rescued Joseph from the pit and the prison, and He blessed him with a palace (Genesis 37–50). He led Moses through the sea (Exodus 14). He helped Joshua knock down a wall (Joshua 6), forgave David for his sins (Psalm 51), and fed thousands with one little boy's lunch (John 6).

God didn't leave any of those people to face their troubles alone—and He won't leave you either!

Lord, thank You for always being there to help me with whatever I need, amen.

TODAY WITH JESUS . . . REMEMBER GOD NEVER LEAVES YOU ALONE.

IT JUST DOESN'T MAKE SENSE!

I remain confident of this: I will see the goodness of the Lord.
PSALM 27:13 NIV

Have you ever faced a problem that didn't make sense and just wouldn't go away? Maybe it was a bully, a struggle with schoolwork, an illness, or a problem at home. Why does God allow such problems to stick around?

If you've ever wondered about that, you're not alone. Before David became king, he spent a long time running from King Saul, who wanted to kill him! God had already promised David he'd be king, so why was it taking so long? David may not have understood the delay, but God knew exactly what He was doing. He was teaching David to trust Him and to be ready for all the battles he'd later face as king.

You see, God uses troubles to make His people stronger (Romans 8:28). So your pesky problem just might be preparing you for something big. Trust God (Proverbs 3:5–6)—one day it will all make sense.

*Lord, when things don't make sense, help
me to trust You anyway, amen.*

**TODAY WITH JESUS . . . TRUST GOD TO
USE TROUBLES TO TEACH YOU.**

TRUST GOD WITH YOUR TROUBLES

Praise God forever and ever. . . . He gives wisdom
to people so they become wise. And . . . He makes
known secrets that are deep and hidden.

DANIEL 2:20–22

D o you trust God with your troubles? Are you willing to do whatever God tells you to do—even if it doesn't make sense? If you are, God will show you amazing things!

That's what He did for Daniel. The evil King Nebuchadnezzar ordered Daniel to tell him what his dream meant—but he wouldn't even tell Daniel what the dream was! And if Daniel couldn't tell him the meaning of the dream Nebuchadnezzar refused to tell him about, Daniel would be killed (Daniel 2). It seemed hopeless. But Daniel trusted God. He told King Nebuchadnezzar, "There is a God in heaven who explains secret things" (v. 28). Then God showed Daniel the dream and all that it meant. Daniel was saved, and God was glorified!

Do you ever face a problem that seems hopeless? Trust God—even when you don't understand—and obey Him. You'll amazed by what He does when you trust Him completely.

Lord, You know my problem. Please show me what to do, amen.

**TODAY WITH JESUS . . . WHEN EVERYTHING
SEEMS HOPELESS, TRUST GOD.**

YOUR HOLY HELPER

I pray that the God who gives hope will fill you with much joy and peace while you trust in him. Then your hope will overflow by the power of the Holy Spirit.
ROMANS 15:13

Every day you have things to do and choices to make. Some are quick and easy, but others are much bigger and harder. Some days you may even wonder, *How in the world will I get through this day?*

Listen to God and His still, small voice as He whispers, *I will get you through* (2 Corinthians 3:5). *I will show you the way to go* (Psalm 32:8). *I will do everything you need* (Psalm 138:8). *Trust Me, I will help you* (Proverbs 3:5–6).

How will God help you today? Through His Holy Spirit—your Holy Helper. When you decide to follow Jesus, the Holy Spirit of God actually comes to live inside you. He helps you by teaching you, guiding you, and making you able to do all God wants you to do. The Spirit stays busy in your life. Look for His work, listen to His quiet whispers, and follow wherever He leads you.

Lord, thank You for Your Holy Spirit. I know that together we can handle anything I have to do today, amen.

TODAY WITH JESUS . . . LOOK FOR THE SPIRIT'S WORK IN YOUR DAY.

FEBRUARY

HEARING GOD

"Today listen to what he says. Do not be stubborn."
HEBREWS 3:7–8

There's more to listening than just having sounds fall into your ears. Truly listening—whether it's to your parents, to a friend, or to God—means being willing to *hear* what's actually being said. And when it comes to listening to God (and your parents), it also means being willing to *do* what He says.

It's easy to listen when God says things like, "I love you," or "Be kind to your friends." But when He says things like, "Love your enemies," or "Forgive that person who said mean things about you" . . . well, that's not so easy.

When you try to listen to God, don't be surprised if He fills your thoughts with something you need to do or change. Pay attention to whatever God has to say, and then do it—remembering that He only wants the very best for you.

Lord, help me to listen and to hear everything
You want to tell me, amen.

**TODAY WITH JESUS . . . HEAR GOD—
AND DO WHAT HE SAYS.**

IT'S SWEETER TO FORGIVE

He has taken our sins away from us as far as the east is from west.
PSALM 103:12

When someone wrongs you, what do you do? Get even? Hurt them back? It's easy to feel that way, but God wants you to forgive—because He forgave you. "But how can I forgive?" you ask. God gives you the way:

- *Say you're sorry to God*: Yes, you may have been wronged, but your unforgiving heart wrongs God. Ask God to forgive you—and then forgive that person too.
- *Let it go*: Stop expecting that person to make it up to you.
- *Understand*: God was hurt by that sin, too, and He'll take care of judging that person—so you don't need to.
- *Remember*: How many times has God forgiven you?

God can't forgive those who won't forgive others. So don't allow an unforgiving heart to make your life bitter or keep you away from God. Forgive—life is so much sweeter when you do.

*Lord, please help me forgive others the
way that You forgive me, amen.*

TODAY WITH JESUS . . . CHOOSE TO FORGIVE.

WHEN YOU'RE AFRAID

When I am afraid, I will trust you. I praise God for his word. I trust God. So I am not afraid. What can human beings do to me?
PSALM 56:3–4

Take a look at that first word in the scripture above. It says *when*— "*When* I am afraid." It doesn't say "*If* I am afraid." King David wrote those words long ago, but they are just as true today. There *will* be times when you're afraid. That's because you live in a fallen world full of sin. But you don't have to face frightening times alone. God will help you, *and* He will use those times to teach you to trust Him, even when you're afraid.

Is there something worrying you today? Or making you afraid? Is there something in your life you just don't think you can handle? Then do what David did: *trust God*. He'll comfort and protect you. He'll take care of your every need in His own perfect way. And He'll never leave you or forget about you (Deuteronomy 31:6, 8). Trust God—He *will* help you.

Lord, when I am afraid, I will trust You to take care of me, amen.

**TODAY WITH JESUS . . . TALK TO GOD
IF YOU'RE WORRIED OR AFRAID.**

JESUS HEALS

All creation was subjected to God's curse. But with eager
hope, the creation looks forward to the day when it will join
God's children in glorious freedom from death and decay.

ROMANS 8:20–21 NLT

Sometimes, when you sit and talk to God, you may remember things from the past—things that hurt you or made you sad. You thought you'd gotten over them, but now you're sad and hurt all over again. It's like bumping a bruise you thought was completely healed and realizing that it still hurts.

Why do those sad memories pop into your thoughts? Because Jesus wants to heal you *completely*—to take away *all* the pain. But before He can do that, Jesus must first touch those painful memories with His light, His love, and His truth. He might show you that you still need to forgive someone—or even to forgive yourself for a past mistake.

Remembering sad and hurtful times can be hard, but trust Jesus. Don't be afraid. Talk to Him, listen, and let Him heal your hurt completely.

Jesus, I trust You to heal all the hurting parts of my life, amen.

**TODAY WITH JESUS . . . TALK TO HIM ABOUT
ANYTHING THAT MAKES YOU SAD.**

TELL GOD

I am always with you. You have held my hand. You guide me
with your advice. And later you will receive me in honor.
PSALM 73:23–24

Are there some troubles you don't want to tell anyone about—not your best friend, not your teacher, maybe not even your mom or dad? Maybe you're embarrassed or afraid or worried about what they might think or say. So you keep those troubles to yourself, and you end up feeling all alone.

But you are *never* alone! When you decide to follow Jesus, the Holy Spirit of God comes to live inside you. And the wonderful thing about God is that He already knows more about that trouble you're facing than you do.

So don't shut God out of your troubles. Sit and talk to Him. Tell Him everything you're thinking and feeling. Ask Him to show you what to do. God is the wisest friend and the most perfect helper you'll ever have. You can trust Him with anything and everything—God will never let you down.

> *Thank You, God, for knowing me so well and for*
> *always being ready to help me, amen.*

**TODAY WITH JESUS . . . SHARE YOUR
TROUBLES WITH GOD.**

BIG ENOUGH AND STRONG ENOUGH

Praise be to the God and Father of our Lord Jesus Christ. In Christ, God has given us every spiritual blessing in heaven.

EPHESIANS 1:3

God is big enough and strong enough to take care of whatever you need today. He never gets tired, He never runs out of blessings, and He never wishes you'd just leave Him alone. God is *always* there for you. When you love and trust Him, He promises to give you every spiritual blessing—wonderful things like love, joy, courage, and peace.

But are *you* ready to let God help and bless you? Or are you afraid to trust Him? Sure, it can be a little scary at first, but give it a try. Start by looking for all the ways God is already working in your life. Believe His promises, and obey His commands—to love Him and to love others.

When you trust God, everything else in your life falls into place—like the pieces of a puzzle. So go ahead and trust Him. He really will take care of you.

Lord, I praise You for being big enough and strong enough to take care of me, amen.

TODAY WITH JESUS . . . TRUST GOD TO TAKE CARE OF YOU.

WHEN GOD SPEAKS

God said, "I will be with you. This will be the proof that I am sending you: . . . all of you will worship me on this mountain."
EXODUS 3:12

When God wanted Moses to lead the Israelites out of slavery in Egypt, He spoke to Moses through a burning bush. Why did God use such an unusual way of speaking? To show that His mighty power would be with Moses and the Israelites as they fled Egypt (Exodus 3). Did God tell Moses every step of His plan? No. But God told Moses just enough so that he could trust and obey Him.

Chances are, God won't speak to you through a burning bush. Instead, He'll most likely speak to you through prayer, the Bible, and the people in your life. And God probably won't show you every step of His plan for you, either. But He'll show you enough that you can trust Him and take the next step He shows you.

The truth is God *wants* you to know Him. He's your Protector, Provider, and King. Listen when He speaks—and follow Him.

Lord, thank You for speaking to me. Help me learn to listen and to follow You, amen.

TODAY WITH JESUS . . . LISTEN FOR WHAT GOD WANTS TO TELL YOU.

THE GREATEST GARDENER

*"He trims and cleans every branch that produces fruit
so that it will produce even more fruit. . . . You cannot
produce fruit alone. You must remain in me."*

JOHN 15:2, 4

If you made a list of all your troubles, sad times, and challenges, you'd probably feel a bit gloomy! But there are a couple of things you should know: First, God allowed each of those things to come into your life for a reason. And second, He'll use them to make you more like Jesus.

So when difficult things come into your life, don't be sad. Don't worry or give up. God hasn't deserted you. Instead, those difficult things are a sign that God believes He can do great things with you.

You see, God is like a gardener—the greatest gardener of all. He knows exactly what you need to grow. A little trim here, and a bit of rain there. Or perhaps He'll plant you in a different spot. Just remember: everything God does is to help you grow bigger and stronger—and more like Jesus.

*Lord, You are the greatest gardener, and I
will trust You to help me grow, amen.*

**TODAY WITH JESUS . . . SEE TOUGH
TIMES AS A CHANCE TO GROW.**

MORE LIKE JESUS

We were made like the man of earth. So we will
also be made like the man of heaven.
1 CORINTHIANS 15:49

There are some things you just can't do all by yourself: forgive your own sins, give yourself peace in tough times, or get yourself into heaven. You need God to do those things for you—and some other things you don't even know you need. So sometimes, God will put people and events in your life to teach you about His goodness or how to follow Him. Because He knows that's what you need.

God doesn't just want you to be happy or healthy or popular—He wants you to be more and more like His Son, Jesus (Romans 8:29).

You may not even know how you need to change to be like Jesus, but God knows because He's the One who made you. So whatever this day brings—joys or troubles—see each event as a chance for God to teach you to be more like His Son.

Lord, thank You for helping me to be more
and more like Jesus, amen.

TODAY WITH JESUS . . . LOOK FOR
WAYS TO BE MORE LIKE HIM.

GOD AT WORK

[God] will support you and keep you from falling.
He is the God who gives all grace.
1 PETER 5:10

God doesn't waste anything—not even troubles. He'll use everything you have to face today to make you stronger and to draw you closer to Him. Remember when David fought off the bear and the lion to protect his sheep? He had lots of practice with his slingshot chasing off those predators. And God used all that practice to get David ready to fight the giant Goliath. That wasn't just luck—that was God at work!

God will use whatever you're facing today too. You may not see how right now, but God is definitely working through your day to make sure you're ready for the days to come.

Remember, God never makes mistakes, and He doesn't do anything without a good reason. When some pesky problem pops up, remember that God will use it for your good. So smile—and thank God for His work in your life.

Father, thank You for using everything in
my life to make me stronger, amen.

TODAY WITH JESUS . . . LOOK FOR WAYS
GOD IS WORKING IN YOUR LIFE.

A LITTLE BIT AT A TIME

"I will force those people out of your land very slowly."
EXODUS 23:30

When problems just won't go away, it can make you feel like giving up. But don't do that! Instead, remember God's promises—and believe them.

When God was getting Israel ready to take over the promised land, He told the people they would face lots of enemies. It would take time to drive them all out. Of course, God could have just spoken a word and made all those enemies disappear. So why didn't He? Why did God slowly remove the enemies a little bit at a time? Because God wanted the Israelites to learn how to trust Him and depend on Him each day.

God works the same way in your life. He uses the problem that just won't go away to teach you to trust and depend on Him. It may seem to take *forever*, but God is working. And learning to trust God will bless you for your entire life.

> *Dear God, I'll trust You to take care of my troubles*
> *in Your own perfect way and time, amen.*

**TODAY WITH JESUS . . . DEPEND ON GOD TO
GET YOU THROUGH YOUR TROUBLES.**

NOT ONE SINGLE THING

I am convinced that nothing can ever separate us from God's love. Neither death nor life, neither angels nor demons, neither our fears for today nor our worries about tomorrow.

ROMANS 8:38 NLT

Have you ever done something or said something so terrible that you thought, *There's no way God still loves me*? If you've ever thought that, then you're wrong. Because there's nothing—not one single thing—you could ever do or say that would make God stop loving you. There's no mistake big enough to mess up God's love for you.

In fact, when you're feeling your absolute worst, completely unworthy, and totally defeated, *that* is when God pulls you closest to Him. Psalm 34:18 promises that, "The Lord is close to the broken-hearted. He saves those whose spirits have been crushed."

The most dangerous thing you can do is to pull away from God. Instead, run to Him in prayer. Tell Him all about your sins and how you've messed up. Ask Him to forgive you and teach you. And then praise Him for loving you so perfectly.

Lord, thank You for loving me so very much—
even when I mess up, amen.

TODAY WITH JESUS . . . REMEMBER
GOD'S LOVE NEVER ENDS.

LET GOD RESCUE YOU

He reached down from heaven and rescued
me; he drew me out of deep waters.
2 SAMUEL 22:17 NLT

Do you ever worry? Do you ever wish God would call you up and just tell you what to do about your troubles? The thing is, you won't see *God* pop up on your caller ID—but you will hear Him whisper, and you have to be ready to listen. When you *don't* listen, sometimes God will actually let your problems get worse—that is, until you're so out of options that you're finally ready to listen to Him, trust His plan, and follow Him.

You see, trusting God and following Him fit together like two pieces of the same puzzle. You must *trust* that God's plan is the absolute best one for you—which means admitting you can't fix it on your own—and then you must *follow* Him.

Until then, you're like a drowning person who struggles and even fights against the One trying to rescue you. Stop fighting God. Instead, trust His power, wisdom, and love. And trust His plan to rescue you.

> *Lord, thank You for rescuing me. Help me trust*
> *Your plan for me and follow it, amen.*

TODAY WITH JESUS . . . FOLLOW GOD'S PLAN.

A PERFECT LOVE

We love because God first loved us.

1 JOHN 4:19

It's easy for your thoughts to get stuck on the relationships that went wrong: the friend who let you down, the big kid who bullied you, the person who lied. And it's easy to understand why the people who hurt you get so much of your attention—because you just want to figure out what went wrong.

But you know what? People will never be perfect. There will always be disappointments and hurts—even from those who love you the most. Only God's love is perfect.

The people around you can care for you, encourage you, and accept you, but only God can truly fill you up with a love that never, ever ends. If your relationship with another person isn't going the way you want, pray for that person. Then turn to God, and ask Him to fill you up with His perfect, never-ending love.

Father, thank You for loving me with a love that will never end, amen.

TODAY WITH JESUS . . . TRY TO LOVE OTHERS THE WAY GOD LOVES YOU.

NOTHING TO FEAR

God's perfect love takes away fear.
1 JOHN 4:18

Do you ever worry about God's love—if God really loves you, or if He'll ever stop loving you? Those kinds of worries fill your heart with fear—fear of getting hurt, of trusting God, even of being rejected by God. And fear keeps you from knowing the amazing joy of God's love.

The truth is that you have *nothing* to fear when it comes to God's love. When you decide to follow Him, He promises, "No one can snatch [you] away from me" (John 10:28 NLT). And He also promises nothing will ever separate you from His love (Romans 8:38–39).

God's love for you will never change or end. He wants you to know that and to enjoy all the wonderful blessings He has for you. So ask Him to show you His love, and let that love chase away all your fears.

Dear God, please show me how much You
love me. Chase away my fears, amen.

TODAY WITH JESUS . . . LOOK FOR GOD'S LOVE.

WHILE YOU WAIT

From long ago no one has ever heard of a God like you. No one has ever seen a God besides you. You help the people who trust you.

ISAIAH 64:4

Have you ever had to wait for God to answer a prayer? You've asked Him for what you want, and you're praying He'll bless you with it, but now you have to wait for His answer. That's when it's easy for scary thoughts to creep in, like, *What if God doesn't want to bless me?* or *What if I've messed up too much?*

That's why Psalm 37:4 (NASB) tells you to "Delight yourself in the LORD; and He will give you the desires of your heart." Of course, that verse doesn't mean that God is like a magic genie—make a wish and get whatever you want. Instead, it means you should think about God and getting to know Him better, instead of thinking about yourself and what you want. Because when you focus on God, the things God wants to bless you with become the things you want. And God's blessings are greater than anything you could ever imagine (Ephesians 3:20)!

Lord, thank You for hearing my prayers. Help me to want the things You want, amen.

TODAY WITH JESUS . . . DO ONE THING JUST TO MAKE GOD SMILE.

WHEN YOU DON'T KNOW WHAT TO DO

Where does my help come from? My help comes
from the Lord. He made heaven and earth.
PSALM 121:1–2

Every day, you'll face challenges. Some will be no problem—you'll know exactly what to do. But for others, you'll have no clue how to tackle them. And those problems that leave you clueless? They will completely take over your thoughts . . . if you let them.

God allows these difficult things to come into your life so that you'll learn to trust Him. Remember, God's goal for you is to make your faith stronger. He does that by creating tough situations that leave you no other choice *except* to trust Him (Romans 8:28).

When you don't know what to do, don't just rush out and try to make up an answer. First, pray as you think about God and the kind of person He wants you to be. Second, take whatever steps you know He has told you to take. Third, trust God to take care of the rest. You won't always know what to do, but God does. Trust Him!

Lord, sometimes I have no idea what I should do, but
I know I can always trust You to guide me, amen.

TODAY WITH JESUS . . . ASK GOD WHEN
YOU DON'T KNOW WHAT TO DO.

GETTING TO KNOW GOD

Truly know me and understand that I am the
LORD who demonstrates unfailing love.
JEREMIAH 9:24 NLT

God *wants* you to get to know Him and what He wants for your life. Sometimes it may feel as if He's far away and not listening to your prayers—especially when you're waiting for an answer. But that's never true—God is always with you and always listening.

The question is: Are you afraid to get to know God? Are you worried He'll think you're not good enough? Or that He'll ask you to do something hard, something you don't want to do? Maybe you're worried He'll ask you to change the way you act, like giving up gossip or changing the friends you hang out with.

Stop worrying! God loves you, no matter what, and He has the most amazing plan for your life. So don't be afraid. Open up God's Word and get to know Him. Because He already knows you—and He loves you.

Lord, I want to get to know You. Please use Your
Word to show me who You are, amen.

TODAY WITH JESUS . . . SPEND TIME
READING GOD'S WORD.

WAITING

*Wait for the Lord's help. Be strong and brave
and wait for the Lord's help.*
PSALM 27:14

It's hard to wait for what you want, especially when you *know* it's coming. Perhaps it's waiting for your birthday or for Christmas morning. Maybe it's waiting for something bigger—like a promised blessing from God.

King David knew about waiting. When David was a young man, God promised to make him king of Israel (1 Samuel 16). But David waited over twenty years and faced lots of hard times before he became king (2 Samuel 5). Why the wait? Because all that waiting brought him closer to God (Psalm 119:71). That's why David was able to say, "Wait for the Lord's help." He knew God would keep His promise, no matter how long it took.

If you're waiting for God to keep a promise, believe that it's coming. God hasn't forgotten, and every moment you wait is a chance to grow closer to Him.

> *Lord, I trust You, and I know You'll always keep
> Your promises. Help me wait on You, amen.*

**TODAY WITH JESUS . . . USE TIMES OF
WAITING TO GROW CLOSER TO GOD.**

PRAISE HIM

Come, let's bow down and worship him. Let's kneel before the Lord who made us. He is our God.

PSALM 95:6–7

Every day is full of good things and not-so-good things. It's tempting to let the not-so-good things take over your thoughts and stress you out. Don't do that. Think about God instead, and how He's able to help you, no matter what you face (Romans 8:37).

Think about who God is, and worship Him. Remember all that He's done for you in the past, and praise Him. Thank Him for sending Jesus to save you and for all the ways He takes care of you, protects you, and loves you. Open up the Bible and read about all the ways God has helped His people. Thank Him for using His power in your life—just as He did for Moses, Abraham, Esther, and Peter. Because when you remember how big God is, then your troubles seem so much smaller. Stay close to God, and nothing will be able to stand against you.

God, You are the most powerful, the most wise, and the most loving, and I praise You, amen.

TODAY WITH JESUS . . . THINK ABOUT THE POWER AND MIGHT OF GOD.

GO AHEAD AND ASK

*All Scripture is inspired by God and is useful for teaching
and for showing people what is wrong in their lives. . . .
the person who serves God will be ready and will have
everything he needs to do every good work.*
2 TIMOTHY 3:16–17

You have questions—about God, the world, yourself, and how you should live. And it's okay to ask those questions. Sometimes God will answer through your prayers or the words of another person. But usually God answers through the Bible—as you read it and think about it.

The Bible isn't just another book; it's God's very own words. And God's Holy Spirit uses those words to teach you and to make you more like Jesus. When you're upset or frightened, He'll lead you to verses of comfort. When you want to give up, He'll remind you of God's promises that give so much hope. He'll guide you with its truths and help you see your sins. All through the Bible, God answers your questions. In fact, He uses those questions to pull you closer to Him. So go ahead and ask . . . then open up His Word for the answers.

*Lord, thank You for Your Word. As I read it, please help
me find Your answers to my questions, amen.*

**TODAY WITH JESUS . . . READ GOD'S WORD
AND LISTEN FOR HIS ANSWERS.**

SAY YES

Lord, I trust you. I have said, "You are my God."

PSALM 31:14

G od wants you to learn to trust Him more and more each day. To help you do that, He may actually challenge you by asking you to do something that's hard.

That's what happened to a widow in the town of Zarephath. There was a terrible drought, and she had only a small bit of flour and oil left to feed herself and her son. It would be their last meal, and then they would starve. But God challenged her to give her flour and oil to His prophet Elijah (1 Kings 17:1–16). It would've been easy to say no— after all, it was all the food they had. But she said yes. And because she obeyed, God made sure her flour and oil did not run out.

One day, God may ask you to give up something important. Trust Him, and say yes—then watch as He blesses you more than you could ever imagine.

*Lord, help me trust You and say yes when You
challenge me to do hard things, amen.*

**TODAY WITH JESUS . . . LOOK FOR GOD'S
CHALLENGES—AND SAY YES.**

GOD WILL HELP

God is our protection and our strength. He
always helps in times of trouble.
PSALM 46:1

God *can* and *will* help you. You don't ever have to worry about that. Your job is to love Him and follow Him with all your heart, mind, soul, and strength. That's easy when everything is going great. But when things aren't so great, it gets a lot harder.

You can believe that God will always do what's best for you—though He may not do it right away. Sometimes He asks you to wait. And sometimes He allows hard times to come into your life. That's because He wants you to learn to trust Him, *especially* when times are tough and you don't understand why.

Keep talking to God and reading His Word. Let His promises fill you with hope. Remember, God never makes a mistake, and He never fails. He can fix any problem you face. Keep trusting Him. He can and will help you—in His own perfect way and time.

> *God, I don't always understand what's happening or*
> *why, but I believe You'll never let me down, amen.*

TODAY WITH JESUS . . . TRUST GOD TO HELP YOU.

LEARNING TO TRUST

Those who know the Lord trust him. He will
not leave those who come to him.

PSALM 9:10

God doesn't always ask you to do easy things. After all, if following God were easy, everyone would do it. The truth is, in some ways, following God will be the hardest thing you will ever do, because it means trusting Him even when it doesn't make sense.

You're human, so you like to be in control. But when you follow God, you must learn to let Him be in control. He understands that's hard for you. But He's a gentle and patient teacher, and He'll help you when you make mistakes.

The thing is, God's help might not look like you think it should. For example, He might teach you to trust Him by giving you a problem you can't fix on your own—a problem only He can fix. If that happens, keep talking to God and reading His Word. Trust Him, and He'll show you the answer when the time is right.

Father, I want to trust You more. Help me see all
the ways You're working in my life, amen.

TODAY WITH JESUS . . . TRUST GOD, ESPECIALLY
WHEN YOU DON'T UNDERSTAND.

WHEN EVERYTHING GOES WRONG

A person may think up plans. But the Lord decides what he will do.
PROVERBS 16:9

Have you ever had a day where *absolutely nothing* goes right? A day when you know what you need to do—go to school, do your chores, hang out with your friends—but from the second you wake up, everything goes wrong?

Don't look at those days as a mistake or a punishment. See them, instead, as a chance to practice trusting God. Let bad days remind you that your life is in God's hands and you can trust Him to take care of you (Proverbs 3:5–6).

No matter what your plans might be for today, God has His own plans. Sometimes they'll agree with yours, but sometimes they won't. When that happens, don't fight God and try to force your own plans to work. Instead, let Him lead you—one step at a time—through your day. It may feel risky and a little scary, but trust God to bring something good out of even your worst day.

Lord, I don't want to fight Your plans for me. Help me follow You even on my worst days, amen.

**TODAY WITH JESUS . . . TRUST GOD'S
PLANS FOR YOUR DAY.**

A HOLY HELPER

"You will not succeed by your own strength or by your own power. The power will come from my Spirit."

ZECHARIAH 4:6

Do you ever worry that you're just not good enough? Or that you're going to fail and fall flat on your face? Believe it or not, *everyone* worries about this. Some people are just better at hiding it than others.

But when you choose to follow Jesus, you never have to worry about your worth again. Why? Because God's Holy Spirit comes to live inside you. Other people can only count on themselves to be successful, but as a child of God, you have a holy helper who makes sure you're accepted, important, and able to do everything God asks you to do (Philippians 2:13). So if something still doesn't work out, you can know it just wasn't God's plan for you. God may even use failure as a way to protect you from something that would be bad for you. Trust God and His plan—He will never let you down.

*Lord, I know You'll help me do all that
You want me to do, amen.*

TODAY WITH JESUS . . . COUNT ON GOD'S HELP.

DON'T GIVE UP

You must hold on, so you can do what God wants
and receive what he has promised.
HEBREWS 10:36

Don't give up. No matter how bad things look or how much you want to just quit—don't. You may not be able to see the sunshine right now because of all the rain, but it's still there. Things will change and your situation will get better . . . if you don't give up.

God could step in at any moment and completely amaze you. He hasn't left you, and He has the perfect answer for all the troubles you're facing. In fact, He'll use those troubles to show you just how big, powerful, and mighty He is. But you can't give up on Him. You can't stop listening to Him and obeying Him. You can't stop doing what's right. Because if you do, you'll miss His wonderful answer.

Wait for God. Let Him make you strong (Psalm 27:13–14). He'll rescue you and reward you if you keep following Him (Galatians 6:9).

God, I'm tired, but I'm not giving up. I'm going to trust
You and wait for Your answer to my troubles, amen.

TODAY WITH JESUS . . . KEEP DOING
WHAT'S RIGHT AND DON'T GIVE UP.

GOD IS BIGGER

You, Lord, give true peace. You give peace to those who depend on you.

ISAIAH 26:3

When your troubles seem bigger than you are, it's easy to start doubting God. After all, you can't see or touch Him, and your problems are right in front of you—they *seem* more real than He does. So you figure, you have to find your own way out of your troubles. But thinking like that will just wear you out and keep you from seeing all the ways God *is* working in your life.

Your problems may seem huge, but remember God is bigger. He promises to take care of you (Psalm 138:8). So talk to Him. Take all your doubts and questions to Him (2 Corinthians 10:5). Then praise Him for all He's already done, and tell Him you trust Him to fix your troubles. Not only will God take away your doubts and fears, but He'll also fill you up with His love and peace (2 Timothy 1:7). So remember, your troubles may be bigger than you, but they're never bigger than God.

*Lord, help me remember that You are big enough
to take care of any trouble I ever face, amen.*

**TODAY WITH JESUS . . . REMEMBER GOD
IS BIGGER THAN ANY PROBLEM.**

MARCH

WATCH AND SEE

*We had great burdens there that were greater than our own
strength. . . . But this happened so that we would not trust
in ourselves. It happened so that we would trust in God.*
2 CORINTHIANS 1:8–9

There will be days when you just cannot handle the troubles that are thrown at you—at least not on your own. And sometimes, the harder you try to fix things, the worse they seem to get!

What should you do? Turn to God. Tell Him all about those troubles and trust Him to fix them. He'll not only help you through them, but He'll use them—like a tool—to shape you into the person He created you to be.

God never meant for you to live life all on your own. He wants you to live life *with Him*. He wants to be there for you and to help you—you just have to let Him. And when you let God into your life, He'll do more with it than you could ever imagine.

So don't be afraid when you face troubles. Trust God. Then watch for the amazing ways He helps you.

> *Jesus, I give all my troubles to You. And I can't
> wait to see how You help me, amen.*

**TODAY WITH JESUS . . . LOOK FOR
THE WAYS GOD HELPS YOU.**

YOU DON'T HAVE TO WORRY

*All people have sinned. . . . People are made right with God
by his grace, which is a free gift. They are made right with
God by being made free from sin through Jesus Christ.*

ROMANS 3:23–24

D o you ever think about your sins? Maybe you've been angry, jealous, or selfish. Or perhaps you've lied, cheated, or talked badly about a friend. Do you ever worry that your sins will keep you out of heaven? After all, the apostle Paul said, "Those who do these things will not be in God's kingdom" (Galatians 5:21). Is it possible that you've done something so bad, so sinful that God just won't forgive you?

No!

Dear child, everyone sins in some way. Your sins don't surprise God. He knows you're going to mess up. That's why He sent Jesus. And when you decide to accept Jesus as your Savior, His blood—the blood He shed on the cross—washes away all your sins. Jesus makes everything between you and God right again. You don't have to worry or be afraid. You just need Jesus.

*Jesus, thank You for washing me clean and
taking away all my sins, amen.*

**TODAY WITH JESUS . . . PRAISE HIM
FOR TAKING AWAY YOUR SINS.**

THE DEVIL'S TRICKS

*The woman saw that the tree was beautiful. She saw
that its fruit was good to eat and that it would make
her wise. So she took some of its fruit and ate it.*
GENESIS 3:6

The Devil is a tricky fellow. He knew Eve wanted wisdom, so he told
her the fruit from the Tree of Knowledge would make her wise.
He'll try to trick you in the same way—by pretending to offer you what
you want. And because the Devil knows *exactly* what you want, he'll
hide the sin inside that thing you want. Then, if the Devil is able to
trick you into sinning, he'll try to make you feel so ashamed that you
hide from God, just as Adam and Eve did in the garden.

First of all, there's no sin so terrible that it would ever make
God stop loving you or wanting you with Him. Secondly, when you
sin—and everyone does—don't hide from God. *Run to Him.* Ask Him
to forgive you—and that's exactly what God will do. Ask Him to help
you never fall for that same trap again—and He'll help guide you away
from it.

*Father God, thank You for loving me so much. I know
that I can always come and talk to You, amen.*

**TODAY WITH JESUS . . . BE ON THE LOOKOUT
FOR THE DEVIL'S TRICKS AND TRAPS.**

TALK TO GOD FIRST

Wisdom begins with respect for the Lord. And understanding begins with knowing God.

PROVERBS 9:10

When you're surrounded by troubles, it's tempting to try to fix them yourself, isn't it? *Don't!* Because only God knows everything about your troubles and the perfect way to fix them.

A man named Gehazi learned that lesson long ago. Gehazi was a servant of the prophet Elisha. When the king of Aram sent his massive army to capture Elisha, Gehazi was terrified. He and his master Elisha were surrounded by soldiers, horses, and chariots.

"Master, what can we do?" Gehazi asked.

Elisha simply prayed, "Lord, open my servant's eyes."

Suddenly Gehazi saw that the Lord's heavenly army was all around them, ready to fight for them. The battle was already won (2 Kings 6:8–19)!

When you're surrounded by troubles, don't count only on what *you* can see and figure out for yourself. Count on God. He's in control, and He'll win the battle for you.

Dear God, only You know everything. Help me remember to talk to You about my troubles first, amen.

TODAY WITH JESUS . . . TELL GOD ABOUT YOUR TROUBLES.

NO

I will say to the Lord, "You are my place of safety and protection. You are my God, and I trust you." God will save you from hidden traps.
PSALM 91:2–3

Nobody likes to hear the word *no*, not even from God. But sometimes, even though you pray and pray for God to answer a certain way, He says no. That's when you have a choice to make: When what you want is different from what God wants, will you accept His answer? Or will you demand your own way?

The first thing to remember is that God loves you more than you can imagine and only wants the very best for you. So when He says no, it's for a very good reason. He may be protecting you from something that would end up hurting you. Or He may be saying no to this thing so that He can bless you with something even better later.

You may not understand right away why God says no, but someday you will. Until then, trust Him—and say yes to God, even when His answer is no.

Jesus, I know You only do what's best for me. Help me trust You, especially when You say no, amen.

TODAY WITH JESUS . . . THANK GOD, EVEN WHEN HIS ANSWER IS NO.

THIS WAY OR THAT WAY?

Depend on the Lord. Trust him, and he will take care of you.

PSALM 37:5

When you have a tough decision to make, what do you do? If you're like most people, you probably start trying to figure out what your choices are. What would happen if you chose this? Or that? Which would be harder or easier?

Those are good questions to ask—until God asks you to just trust Him and make the hard choice. It might be the one that doesn't make sense to you. Or it might be the one with bigger challenges—challenges you know you can't handle by yourself. That's when faith has to step in, and you just have to trust God to get you through.

The wonderful thing about trusting God with your decisions is that He'll take you places and show you things you've never even dreamed of. Don't miss out—trust and obey God, and then look for His amazing power to work in your life.

Lord, I know You'll never lead me the wrong way. I will follow You always, amen.

TODAY WITH JESUS . . . ASK GOD TO GUIDE YOUR DECISIONS.

I'M SORRY, GOD

*Being sorry in the way God wants makes a person
change his heart and life. This leads to salvation.*
2 CORINTHIANS 7:10

When you mess up and sin, you need to tell God you're sorry. But that's not all you need to do. God also wants you to *repent*, which is a fancy word that means three things:

1. *Recognize* what you did was actually a sin. You learn about what God calls *sin* when you read the Bible.
2. *Agree* with God that you sinned. If you don't agree with God that you were wrong, then you're not really sorry. It's like apologizing for yelling at your brother or sister—not because you're sorry, but because you don't want to get in trouble.
3. *Turn away* from that sin. Choose to obey God and to not do that sin again. The amazing thing is that God will actually help you obey Him.

So, yes, when you sin, tell God how very sorry you are—but then *repent* and follow Him.

*Lord, I see now that what I did was wrong. Please forgive
me and help me to obey You from now on, amen.*

TODAY WITH JESUS . . . ADMIT WHEN YOU'RE WRONG.

WHO IS GOD?

I am guiding you in wisdom. And I am leading you to do what is right.

PROVERBS 4:11

Who is God to you? Is He like a distant force to you? The Ruler of the universe? The Creator of everything? The One who forgives your sins? Because God wants to be much more. He wants to be close to you—your protector, guide, comforter, strength, and loving Father. He wants to love you and lead you along paths that will stretch your faith and help you grow to look more and more like His Son.

Whatever God allows to happen in your life—good things or even bad things—*everything* is to help you grow closer to Him. So when you face tough times, it's because God wants you to come to Him for help. Pray, study His Bible, and listen to His Holy Spirit as He whispers to your heart.

No one will ever love you as much as God. Trust Him to lead you where you need to go.

*Lord, use everything that happens in my
life to pull me closer to You, amen.*

**TODAY WITH JESUS . . . TURN TO GOD
IN GOOD TIMES AND BAD.**

ABOUT YOU

Thanks be to God, who always leads us in victory through Christ.
2 CORINTHIANS 2:14

How do you talk to yourself . . . about yourself? Do you say things like, "I'm just no good at anything," or "Why would God love me?" Maybe you say things like, "Nobody wants to be my friend," or "I mess up everything." And maybe you have messed up or been hurt by someone. But here's the truth: that isn't how God sees you. When you decide to follow Jesus, He makes you a new creation (2 Corinthians 5:17). No matter what's happened in the past, God gives you a fresh start.

God loves you so much that He sent His Son to save you and His Holy Spirit to live inside you. So stop putting yourself down. After all, God thinks you're so amazing that He wants to adopt you as His very own child (1 John 3:1).

Lord, thank You for loving me so much. Help
me see myself the way You do, amen.

TODAY WITH JESUS . . . DISCOVER HOW
MUCH GOD LOVES YOU IN 1 JOHN 3:1.

BEFORE THE BATTLE BEGINS

We fight with weapons that are different from those the world uses. Our weapons have power from God.

2 CORINTHIANS 10:4

What are your weak spots? You know, those things you know are wrong, but are just so hard to resist. Is gossip one of them? Being greedy or unkind, jealous or angry? Decide *now* how you'll stand up to those temptations. Because if you wait until you're tempted, you'll almost always give in and sin. Defend yourself *before* the battle begins.

First, figure out what kinds of thoughts run through your head when you're tempted. Do you feel unimportant and that tempts you to put someone else down? Do you feel unworthy and that makes you jealous of what others have?

Second, do what Jesus did! When Satan tempted Him, Jesus used God's words to beat him. Feel unworthy? Remember God says you're His child (1 John 3:1). Feel unimportant? Don't forget God says He's got a plan for you (Jeremiah 29:11). Use God's words—and send the Devil running every time (James 4:7).

Lord, please fill my mind and heart with Your words so that I can defend myself against the Devil, amen.

TODAY WITH JESUS . . . REMEMBER YOU BELONG TO GOD.

A REASON FOR YOUR TROUBLES

Do not be surprised at the painful things you are now suffering. These things are testing your faith.
1 PETER 4:12

Do your troubles ever seem so terrible that you wonder if God has forgotten you? Why would He let such awful problems come into your life?

Don't give up. God has *not* forgotten you. In fact, He's right there beside you. And He has a reason for letting you go through all those struggles: so you'll get to know Jesus your Savior better and be more like Him. God actually uses your struggles to help you grow in the fruit of His Spirit—love, joy, peace, patience, kindness, goodness, faithfulness, gentleness, and self-control (Galatians 5:22–23).

When you're struggling, the good news is that Jesus knows exactly how you feel (Hebrews 2:17) because Jesus had troubles, too. He knows how to comfort and guide you. So trust Him and let Him give you His joy—especially in the middle of your troubles.

Lord, I'll trust You to take care of me through whatever troubles I face, amen.

TODAY WITH JESUS . . . TAKE YOUR TROUBLES TO GOD, AND LET HIM COMFORT YOU.

GOD WILL ANSWER

When all the people saw this, they fell down to the ground.
They cried, "The Lord is God! The Lord is God!"

1 KINGS 18:39

When it comes to God, you either believe or you don't. There's no halfway. You have to choose: either trust God and believe He's always with you, or give in and believe you're completely on your own.

The prophet Elijah believed he could always count on God. To prove it, he dared 850 prophets of the phony gods Baal and Asherah to pray for their gods to send down fire from heaven. Whoever sent fire—their false gods or Elijah's one true God—would be Lord of All. Elijah stood up for the God he believed in, and God sent fire (1 Kings 18).

God would not let Elijah down—and He won't let you down either. It may look as if there's no way out of the trouble you're facing. But God will not only make a way—He'll use that problem to show you that He's the one true God!

Lord, I know You are God! And I will trust
You to answer my prayers, amen.

TODAY WITH JESUS . . . BELIEVE GOD IS LORD OF ALL.

GOD WANTS TO LISTEN

You want me to be completely truthful. So teach me wisdom.
PSALM 51:6

Do you ever wonder if you should talk to God about something? Are there problems you're afraid to tell Him about, maybe because you think they're too big or too small or too embarrassing?

You can stop wondering about that because God *wants* you to tell Him absolutely *everything*! God wants you to know that His love for you will never, ever end or fail you—no matter what you tell Him. He cares about the things that worry you. You can come to Him and be completely honest.

After all, God already knows everything you're thinking and feeling. But when you tell Him those things, you're also showing Him that you trust Him with the secrets of your heart. So talk to God—He wants to listen.

Father, thank You for always listening, no
matter what I have to say, amen.

TODAY WITH JESUS . . . FIND A QUIET
PLACE TO TALK TO GOD.

YOUR HEAVENLY FATHER

We have all had fathers here on earth who disciplined us . . . But
God disciplines us to help us, so we can become holy as he is.
HEBREWS 12:9–10 NCV

Some people have great dads here on earth. Others have not-so-great dads. But no matter what kind of dad you have on earth, you have a heavenly Father who loves, protects, and takes care of you. He'll never leave you, reject you, or let you down. When you decide to follow Jesus, you're adopted into God's family. He sends His Holy Spirit to live inside you as proof of His never-ending love for you (Ephesians 1:13–14).

To understand how wonderful this is, you'll have to change your way of thinking—and you'll need help to do that. That's why God allows certain things—like troubles—into your life. He uses those things to show you who He really is, how much He loves you, and how you really can trust Him to take care of you.

No matter how great or not-so-great your earthly dad is, you have a heavenly Father who's perfect.

Father, thank You for adopting me into Your
family. I'm so glad I'm Your child, amen.

TODAY WITH JESUS . . . TRUST GOD TO BE
YOUR PERFECT AND LOVING FATHER.

YOU NEED GOD

"If you come back to me and trust me, you will be saved.
If you will be calm and trust me, you will be strong."
ISAIAH 30:15

You need God. It's just a fact. There's an empty place deep inside you—inside everyone—only God can fill. The problem is you often pretend you *don't* need Him.

Maybe you're trying to do it all on your own so you can prove to God how good you are, or so He'll be pleased with you. But the truth is you can't do it all on your own. And you don't have to prove you're "good enough" for God. He loves you simply because you're you. There's nothing you can do to make God love you more—or less. His love for you is perfect and without end. And what He most wants is for you to trust Him to take care of you

So turn to Him—in good times, in troubled times, and in every time between. Listen to His words and obey His commands. Let God take care of you.

Lord, I know I need You. Please teach me how
to rest and let you take care of me, amen.

TODAY WITH JESUS . . . REMEMBER GOD
LOVES YOU JUST BECAUSE YOU'RE YOU.

ONE STEP AT A TIME

He gives me new strength. For the good of his
name, he leads me on paths that are right.

PSALM 23:3

Have you ever tried to walk through a dark room? You have to move carefully, one step at a time, so you don't stumble and fall. Sometimes life can be like a dark room—filled with choices, troubles, and struggles. You have to move carefully so you don't stumble and fall. The good news is that God is there to guide you through the darkness, one step at a time.

It may seem like others already have all the answers, or their path isn't as dark or as hard as yours. Don't let that worry or upset you. God gives each person just the right path to follow—to shape them into the person He created them to be.

So trust Him. Follow Him. Obey Him when He shows you the next step to take. He'll bring you safely through the darkness and fill your life with His beautiful light (Ephesians 3:20).

Father, thank You for guiding me through dark
times. Help me to shine with Your light, amen.

TODAY WITH JESUS . . . ASK GOD TO
GUIDE YOU THROUGH YOUR DAY.

FORGET THE WHAT-IFS

"Be strong and brave. Be sure to obey all the teachings my servant Moses gave you. If you follow them exactly, you will be successful in everything you do."
JOSHUA 1:7

You never have to worry that you're not "good enough." Why? Because God created you—and He is always right by your side, ready to help you.

Joshua knew that, but he still faced a lot of what-ifs. When Moses died, it was Joshua's job to lead the Israelites into the promised land. But *what if* the people didn't trust Joshua the way they had trusted Moses? *What if* he couldn't handle the challenges? *What if* Joshua couldn't hear God the way Moses had? *What if* he completely failed?

Joshua could have easily been frozen with fear. But he wasn't—because he listened to God's words and trusted Him to lead the way.

And you can do the same thing. God put you where you are for a reason. So forget the what-ifs. Trust God. It's His job to lead you to victory, and it's your job to follow.

*Lord, I believe You will lead me to victory,
so I will follow You, amen.*

WHAT DO YOU BELIEVE?

Remember your promise to me, your servant. It gives me hope.
PSALM 119:49

Are you often worried or upset? Do even tiny troubles ruin your day? If so, maybe it's time to take a look at what you believe about God. Because *what* you believe shapes *how* you see the things that happen in your life.

For example, if you think you can mess up so badly that God will *never* let you into heaven, it's hard to trust Him. You'll always be worried about earning His love and forgiveness. But if you accept that God promises to forgive you when you come to Him (1 John 1:9), and nothing can ever separate you from His love, you'll stop worrying (Romans 8:38–39).

That's why it's so important to know what you believe—and to make sure what you believe matches up with God's Word. Fill your mind with Scripture. Read, study, and think about it. Let it set you free from your worries.

Lord, thank You for Your Word and the hope it gives me, amen.

**TODAY WITH JESUS . . . LEARN ONE
NEW THING FROM GOD'S WORD.**

THE MOST IMPORTANT WORDS

Lord, your word is everlasting. . . . I will never forget your orders because you have given me life by them.
PSALM 119:89, 93

Have you heard the old saying, "Sticks and stones may break my bones, but words can never hurt me"? Don't believe it! Words are powerful. They can build you up or cut you down like a knife. But here's an important truth to remember: no matter what anyone says about you—good or bad—it's never as important or as truthful as what God's Word says about you.

When you read the Bible, you'll learn amazing things—like who God is and how much He loves you. You'll learn that you're His creation and His own adopted child and that you can trust Him always. And you'll discover how to live a life that makes Him smile.

There are no words more important than those found in the Bible. So make them the most important words in your life—and God will bless you through His Words.

Lord, open up Your Word to me and teach me who You are and who I am, amen.

TODAY WITH JESUS . . . READ PSALM 139 TO DISCOVER WHO YOU ARE TO GOD.

LET HIM HAVE CONTROL

*A person's steps are directed by the Lord. How then
can anyone understand their own way?*

PROVERBS 20:24 NIV

G od wants you to trust Him. Not just a little, not even a lot. God wants you to trust Him *completely*. In fact, God wants you to trust Him so much that you don't worry or question His plans for you, even when things aren't going your way. Because God *does* have great plans for you. You just have to ask yourself, *Am I willing to let God be in charge of my life? Will I accept whatever He places in my day—even if I don't like it or it doesn't make sense?*

Perhaps you think you have to hold everything together, or it'll all fall apart. But that only shows how little you understand God. It's possible that everything is falling apart, because *you're* trying to hold it together—instead of letting God take care of it.

God promises to help you, make you strong, and support you (Isaiah 41:10). Don't miss out on His blessings because you're afraid to let Him have control.

*Lord, please help me to trust You and let
You be in charge of my life, amen.*

**TODAY WITH JESUS . . . READ ISAIAH
41:10 AND LET GOD BE IN CHARGE.**

GOD'S WORD

God's word is alive and working. . . . And God's word
judges the thoughts and feelings in our hearts.
HEBREWS 4:12

Every word of the Bible is true. Every single one. So if you hear something that doesn't agree with what the Bible says—about God, yourself, or how to live—toss it out. Get rid of it. Don't let it be part of your life.

Why? Because God's Word is your shield—it protects you from the Devil's lies. The Bible tells you who you are as a child of God. It tells you how to live and how to make wise choices. And it helps you see what is truth and what is a lie.

So if you're wrestling with a big decision, need help with a problem, or simply need to be reassured that you are loved . . . open up your Bible. Search for God's answers. Ask your mom, dad, pastor, or someone you trust to help you. Let God's Word guide you—it'll never steer you wrong.

Father God, please guide me with Your Word so that
I'll know what is true and what is not, amen.

TODAY WITH JESUS . . . LET GOD'S
WORD BE YOUR SHIELD.

BE STILL

"Be still and know that I am God."

PSALM 46:10

The words "be still" probably make you think about sitting quietly without moving. But with God, it means more. It means to stop struggling, to stop worrying and wrestling with your troubles. *Be still* and know that God is greater than any trouble, worry, or fear.

Remember all the promises God made to His people—to Moses, Abraham, Mary, and Peter? He kept every one. And He'll keep His promises to you too. When the Israelites were trapped between the Red Sea and the Egyptian army, their situation looked hopeless, but their instructions were clear: "The LORD will fight for you; you need only to be still" (Exodus 14:14 NIV). And what did God do? The impossible—He blew back the sea and saved His people!

God wants to rescue you from everything that troubles you, but first you must stop struggling. *Be still . . .* and know that God is working in your life.

God, I know You are Lord of All and that You
are all I need. I love You, amen.

**TODAY WITH JESUS . . . READ PROVERBS
3:5–6 AND BE STILL WITH GOD.**

WHEN YOU'RE SURROUNDED

"Don't be afraid or discouraged. . . . The battle
is not your battle. It is God's battle."
2 CHRONICLES 20:15

Do you ever feel as if you're trapped and surrounded? Sometimes it can feel like troubles are coming at you from every side—troubles with friends, at home, at school. One trouble would be tough enough on its own, but all of them together are completely overwhelming!

That's probably how King Jehoshaphat from the Bible felt. Three different armies were marching against him. Just one army would've been too much, but defending his kingdom against all three was impossible! So Jehoshaphat did the very best possible thing: he prayed. And God showed Jehoshaphat that the battle would be won, but not with weapons or plans. It would be won with songs and praise (2 Chronicles 20).

When you're surrounded by troubles, don't start planning how you'll fight. After all, it's not really your battle. Stop and pray instead. Listen to God, obey His Word, and then praise Him for the amazing way He'll rescue you.

> *Lord, thank You for fighting my battles for me. You*
> *are always good and powerful and wise, amen.*

TODAY WITH JESUS . . . PRAISE GOD
WHEN YOU'RE FACING TROUBLES.

IT'S NOT FAIR!

The LORD will work out his plans for my life—for
your faithful love, O LORD, endures forever.

PSALM 138:8 NLT

I t's just not fair!" Have you ever said that? Well . . . you're right. Sometimes life isn't fair. People who do wrong seem to win, and, even though you're trying to do what's right, you still end up with troubles. You wonder why, and you may even ask, "Does God still love me? Why won't He help me?"

When life isn't fair, it hurts. But God uses your hard times to train you to be a better worker for His kingdom. Remember, Abraham spent a hundred years watching other families have children before he had Isaac. Joseph spent years as a slave and in jail before he became a ruler. Paul was beaten, shipwrecked, and thrown in prison, yet today his words still tell others about Jesus.

When life isn't fair, don't give up. And never doubt God's love. Keep doing what's right . . . and watch for the blessings His training brings.

Lord, when things don't seem fair, I'll trust You
and look for Your blessings, amen.

TODAY WITH JESUS . . . LOOK FOR THE
BLESSINGS WHEN LIFE ISN'T FAIR.

24 HOURS

Teach us how short our lives really are so that we may be wise.
PSALM 90:12

Time is more valuable than gold or silver, and so often there doesn't seem to be enough of it. There's so much to juggle—school, homework, chores, sports, hobbies, friends, and family. Because you only have so much time in a day, how you spend that time says a lot about what's important to you. So what about God? Where does He fit in your day?

For example: Do you have plenty of time for playing games on your tablet or phone, but not enough time to read your Bible? Do you spend hours at a ballgame, but never quite make it to church? Do you have time for television, but not time to pray? Are your Saturdays for shopping or serving?

You have twenty-four hours each day—that's 1,440 minutes. How many of those minutes do you give to God? Do they show how much you love God? Make time for God today.

> *Lord, teach me to use my time in a way*
> *that makes You smile, amen.*

**TODAY WITH JESUS . . . ASK GOD HOW
YOU SHOULD SPEND YOUR TIME.**

YOUR PROTECTOR AND DEFENDER

"No weapon that is used against you will defeat you."

ISAIAH 54:17

Some days, the whole world seems to be against you. Perhaps a bully is threatening you, or mean girls are talking about you behind your back. Maybe you stood up for someone who needed help, but now you're the target too. Or maybe you tried to tell someone about Jesus, and now they're laughing at you.

Don't give up—put your life and all these troubles in God's hands. He's your protector and defender. If He's allowed difficult things into your life, that means He's going to use them to make you and your faith stronger.

Remember God's promise: "They will fight against you. But they will not defeat you. . . . I am with you, and I will save you!" (Jeremiah 1:19). Nothing and no one can ever defeat God. Trust Him to take care of every hard thing in your life . . . and to bring something beautiful from them.

Lord, I will trust You, because I know that nothing
and no one can ever defeat You! Amen.

TODAY WITH JESUS . . . DO THE RIGHT THING, NO MATTER WHAT.

MORE THAN OKAY

But in all these things we are completely victorious through God who showed his love for us.
ROMANS 8:37 NCV

S ometimes you just need to know that everything's going to be okay, or that this trouble will be over one day, or that God really *is* working in your life. Dear child, no matter what you're facing, everything will be okay. Not only will you get through this hard time, but God will make you "completely victorious."

Remember Joseph? His brothers sold him as a slave, and he was thrown into prison, even though he'd done nothing wrong. But God used those hard times to train Joseph for his next job—ruler over all Egypt, second only to Pharaoh (Genesis 39–50). If Joseph hadn't gone to prison, he never would've made it to the palace.

When your life feels like a prison of troubles, keep your eyes on the palace that God has waiting for you. He'll make everything more than okay—and He'll make you completely victorious.

Lord, I'm going to trust You to make everything more than okay, amen.

TODAY WITH JESUS . . . REMEMBER JOSEPH, AND TRUST GOD TO TAKE CARE OF YOUR TROUBLES.

DO!

Don't just listen to God's word. You must do what it says.

When you want to be closer to God, it's tempting to think you need to work harder, do more, and serve more. But that's not how you get closer to God. Yes, you *do* need to obey God and serve Him, but not to *make* Him love you more. He already loves you perfectly. Work for God *simply because you love Him*.

If you want to get closer to God, here's how: Read His Word. Talk to Him about it. Then do what His Word says.

Remember, God knows exactly what you need to grow closer to Him. And He gives it to you through His Word, in a prayer, through the words of others. You'll feel it when it happens—a Bible verse or someone's words instantly touch your heart and make you think. But don't just feel and think—*do*! Take that teaching from God and then go out and apply it.

*Lord, show me what I need to learn—and
then, please, help me do it, amen.*

**TODAY WITH JESUS . . . READ MATTHEW
22:39 AND THEN DO IT.**

JESUS UNDERSTANDS

For this reason Jesus had to be made like his brothers
and sisters in every way. . . . so he could be their
merciful and faithful high priest in service to God.
HEBREWS 2:17

Do you ever wish someone understood how you felt? Jesus does. All those struggles you're facing? He faced them too. Jesus was rejected, laughed at, and betrayed by His friends. He knew what it was like to lose someone He loved. He experienced sadness and pain. There's nothing you'll ever face that Jesus doesn't understand. In fact, that's why He came to earth—to experience everything you go through, even the pain (Matthew 9:36).

Before Jesus went to the cross, He went to the Garden of Gethsemane to pray. Jesus knew He needed to go to the cross to save His people. But He also knew it would be terrible, so He went to His Father for the comfort, wisdom, and strength He needed—not just once, but three times.

When you're struggling, go to Jesus. He loves you, and He understands. Go to Him anytime you need Him—He'll be there.

> *Jesus, I'm so sorry for all that You suffered. But I'm*
> *so thankful You understand when I suffer, amen.*

TODAY WITH JESUS . . . REMEMBER
THAT HE UNDERSTANDS.

FROM JESUS

"The only power you have over me is the power given to you by God."

JOHN 19:11

Nothing comes into your life without God's permission—not even troubles.

Jesus taught this truth to Pilate, the Roman governor, just before He went to the cross. Pilate thought *he* was the one who had power over Jesus—the authority to set Him free or send Him to the cross (John 19:10). But Jesus said, "The only power you have over me is the power given to you by God."

Sometimes it seems that another person is to blame for your troubles. But the fact is, God allowed those troubles into your life for a reason: to teach you to trust Him. Remember that Jesus gave His life to save yours, so you really can trust Him with your life. When you do, you'll be amazed at the wonderful ways He works in you and for you.

Lord, help me see my troubles as an opportunity to trust You more, amen.

TODAY WITH JESUS . . . THINK LESS ABOUT YOUR TROUBLES AND MORE ABOUT JESUS.

HE CHOSE TO GO

Christ died for us while we were still sinners. In this way God shows his great love for us.
ROMANS 5:8

Do you ever struggle to believe that God really loves you? If you do, it's time to think about the cross. Jesus didn't have to go to the cross. He didn't have to be arrested, laughed at, or spat on. He didn't have to be beaten or nailed to that wooden cross.

Jesus *chose* to go to the cross. Why? Because it was the only way to save you from your sins. Jesus loves you so much He suffered through the cross for you (John 10:17–18). There's nothing you can do to earn that love or lose it. It's simply His gift to you (Ephesians 2:8–9).

So if you're afraid you've done something so terrible that God won't forgive you, stop worrying. He loves you at your very best and your very worst. You can't stop God from loving you . . . but you can praise Him by giving Him your very best.

Jesus, thank You for loving me so much that
You chose to go to the cross, amen.

TODAY WITH JESUS . . . THINK ABOUT THE CROSS AND HOW HUGE JESUS' LOVE IS.

APRIL

NEVER ALONE

"You believe because you see me. Those who believe without seeing me will be truly happy."
JOHN 20:29

When you're in the middle of a big problem, it's only natural to feel alone, helpless, and even hopeless. But remember this: *you are never alone!* And even though things may look hopeless, it's so very important that you believe God—your all-powerful deliverer—is with you and working in your life always (Deuteronomy 31:8).

Jesus' disciples are the perfect example. Even though Jesus had told them that He was going to the cross, they didn't understand. So when they saw Him die, they felt alone, helpless, and hopeless. But three days later, when Jesus rose from the dead, He gave them a new hope and a faith stronger than ever before.

He'll do the same for you. God won't always take away your problems, but He'll always be there to comfort you with His Word and His presence. So don't give up . . . you're never alone. And when God does His work in your situation, He'll give you a new hope and stronger faith too.

> *Lord, thank You for never leaving me. I'll trust You to bring hope to even my biggest problems, amen.*

TODAY WITH JESUS . . . BELIEVE HE IS WITH YOU.

JESUS' GREAT LOVE

We were spiritually dead because of the things we did wrong against God. But God gave us new life with Christ.

EPHESIANS 2:5

Jesus, the Son of God, *chose* to die on the cross for you. Just think about that: Jesus could have said no. After all, crucifixion was the most horrible way to die. It was completely humiliating and terribly painful. It was the death given to only the worst criminals. But there was something even more painful for Jesus than the shame or the beatings or the nails. For the first time in all eternity, Jesus was separated from God, His Father. *That* was His greatest suffering.

Why would Jesus choose that kind of death? The answer is simple: because that's how much He loves you. Jesus would rather suffer through the cross than be separated from you.

So the next time you're feeling unloved or not good enough, remember all that Jesus did . . . because He loves you and wants you by His side forever.

Jesus, sometimes it's hard to believe You chose to die on the cross to save me. But I'm so very grateful that You did, amen.

TODAY WITH JESUS . . . REMEMBER ALL HE WENT THROUGH JUST TO BE WITH YOU.

TEAR DOWN THE WALL

If we are not faithful, he will still be faithful,
because he must be true to who he is.
2 TIMOTHY 2:13

Do you ever worry you'll mess up so badly that God will just turn away from you? That He'll say, "Forget it. I'm done with this kid"? Well, here are a couple of truths to remember: First, God won't ever turn away from you. And, second, you don't have to be perfect for Him to love you. Does that mean you don't have to obey Him? Of course not! But He understands that you'll mess up sometimes—and He doesn't love you any less for it.

Even though your sins don't change God's love, they *do* build a wall between you and Him. And when shame tempts you to hide your sins from God (which is impossible), that wall gets even higher. So when you sin, confess—tell it to God. Confession tears down the wall, and God promises to forgive you (1 John 1:9). That's how huge His love for you is!

> *Lord, I'm so sorry that I _____. Please forgive*
> *me and help me do better today, amen.*

GOD KEEPS HIS PROMISES

Our Lord Jesus Christ. . . . gave us a new life. He gave us
a living hope because Jesus Christ rose from death.

1 PETER 1:3

When Jesus died and was buried in the tomb, His disciples were crushed. Even though Jesus had promised to come back to them, they didn't understand how He could keep that promise. But He did.

When you're struggling with a terrible sadness or a huge problem, do you find it hard to trust God's promises? If so, remember these lessons from Jesus' resurrection:

1. Just when it seems hopeless, God shows you how awesome His power is.
2. God *always* wins. Nothing stops Him.
3. Nothing—not even death—will ever change God's love for you.

If God can raise Jesus up from the grave, He can certainly take care of anything you have to face. Don't give up—God will keep His promises.

Dear Lord, You're strong enough to beat death, so I
know You can beat any troubles I have, amen.

TODAY WITH JESUS . . . READ MATTHEW
6:25–26 AND BELIEVE.

NOTHING'S TOO BIG FOR GOD

*God has made this promise come true for us. God
did this by raising Jesus from death.*
ACTS 13:33

Jesus' empty grave is an amazing reminder that God always keeps His promises. In fact, there's nothing—not even death or a grave—that can stop God from keeping His promises (Isaiah 55:11).

Jesus died on the cross to defeat sin. Then He rose up from the grave to defeat death. Because of Jesus, sin and death—your two greatest enemies—are defeated. When you decide to follow Jesus, you become a child of God and Jesus gives *you* that victory over sin and death, too. They have no power over you. You're completely forgiven, and you'll live with God in heaven forever.

Is there anything that can keep God from keeping His promises to you? *No!* If sin and death couldn't stop God, then there's no trouble you'll ever face that's too big for Him. Trust God—He'll never let you down.

*Dear Lord, there is nothing too big for You to handle. Thank
You for using Your mighty power to save me, amen.*

TODAY WITH JESUS . . . TRUST GOD'S MIGHTY POWER.

BELIEVING WITHOUT SEEING

"Stop doubting and believe."

JOHN 20:27

When Jesus rose from the grave, He went to His disciples. They saw Him—and they believed. But Thomas wasn't there. He didn't see Jesus, so he didn't believe. Though the others told him they'd seen Jesus with their own eyes, Thomas refused to believe Jesus was alive until he touched His scarred hands and side (John 20:25). Can you imagine how embarrassed Thomas was when Jesus appeared and gave him the proof he'd asked for?

There's a lesson to learn from Thomas: when God makes a promise, He'll keep it—even though He may ask you to wait for it. You may get tired of waiting, and you may ask God for signs, like Thomas did. But Jesus said, "Those who believe without seeing me will be truly happy" (John 20:29).

So stop doubting and *believe*. Trust that God is able to do what He promises—and one day, you'll *see* those promises come true.

Lord, I do believe You'll keep Your promises. Please help me keep believing even when I don't see, amen.

TODAY WITH JESUS . . . READ DEUTERONOMY 7:9 AND BELIEVE GOD KEEPS HIS PROMISES.

THE BEST WAY

Is there someone who worships the Lord? The
Lord will point him to the best way.
PSALM 25:12

S ometimes, life feels as if all you're doing is making one decision after the other. Some are small, everyday decisions—like what to wear or what to eat for a snack. Others are bigger—*much bigger*—like how to help a friend or what to do when someone gets very sick. Thankfully, you never have to make any decision all by yourself because God is always there to guide you through prayer and His Word.

But remember this: when God shows you what to do, He expects you to actually do it. God's Word even says, "Wisdom begins with respect for the Lord. Those who obey his orders have good understanding" (Psalm 111:10). That means you need to obey God—even if His way isn't what *you* want to do.

If you have a decision to make today—and who doesn't?—talk to God. He'll show you the very best way.

> *Lord, Your answers are perfect, so help me listen*
> *to what You say—and then obey, amen.*

TODAY WITH JESUS . . . ASK HIM WHAT YOU SHOULD DO.

OUT OF THE PIG PEN

"'My son . . . was lost, but now he is found!'
So they began to celebrate."

LUKE 15:24

The Bible tells about a boy who took his father's money, left home, and went to a faraway city. There, he lived a life filled with sin. When the money ran out, his "friends" deserted him. He took a job feeding pigs—and he was so desperate and hungry, he wished he could eat the pigs' food!

At last, the boy decided to go home. He was so ashamed, he just hoped his father would take him in as a servant. But when the father saw his lost son coming, he ran to him and hugged him. The father forgave him and welcomed him home as his son.

Your heavenly Father is just like that father. No matter what you do or how far away you wander, He's ready to welcome you back. So when you mess up, run back to the Father. He'll lift you out of your "pig pen" of sin and welcome you home.

Lord, if I've wandered away from You, show me
and help me come back home to You, amen.

TODAY WITH JESUS . . . READ ALL ABOUT
THE LOST SON IN LUKE 15:11–32.

GOD WILL RESCUE YOU

My eyes are always on the LORD, for he rescues me.
PSALM 25:15 NLT

When troubles come charging into your life like an angry bull or a runaway train, what should you do? Begin with these things:

1. Remember how God has helped you in the past.
2. Ask yourself if you're trying to fix everything the way *you* want it, or if you're listening to God.
3. Don't give up! God won't ever leave you or let you down. Listen to Him and obey.
4. Trust that God has a very good reason for everything He allows to touch your life—even troubles. Look for the blessings He will create out of your troubles.
5. Depend on God's mighty power to get you through. He created this entire universe and everything in it, so He can surely take care of you.

Trust God and obey Him—He will always rescue you.

Jesus, please help me to remember that when troubles come, I can count on You, amen.

TODAY WITH JESUS . . . TALK TO HIM WHILE
YOU LOOK UPWARD TODAY, THANK HIM
FOR RESCUING YOU FROM TROUBLE.

PERFECTLY KEPT PROMISES

*Delight yourself in the L*ORD*; and He will give*
you the desires of your heart.

PSALM 37:4 NASB

A promise is only as good as the one who makes it. When it comes to God's promises, there's no question He'll do exactly what He says (Joshua 21:45).

One of God's promises is that if you love Him and delight yourself in Him, He'll give you what your heart truly desires. You see, God doesn't want you just to *serve Him*—He wants you to *know Him* because that fills your life with meaning and joy.

When you make God your joy, He will keep His promise to give you what you truly want. But understand that "what you want" may come in a surprising way or a bigger way than you ever imagined. Or it may change completely as you learn to love and want the things God loves and wants. But one thing you can know for sure: God will keep His promise *perfectly* because that's who He is (1 Kings 8:56).

Lord, please help me to love and want the
things You love and want, amen.

TODAY WITH JESUS . . . LOVE WHAT GOD LOVES.

WAIT FOR AN ANSWER

Don't worry about anything; instead, pray about everything. Tell God what you need, and thank him for all he has done.
PHILIPPIANS 4:6 NLT

Do you ever get tired of waiting for God to answer a prayer? You know He *will* answer. He *always* answers—in the perfect way and in the perfect time—but sometimes it's hard to wait on Him. It's tempting to just rush out and do what you think is right. Don't do that! You'll only make things worse. Keep trusting God, and He will answer you *perfectly*.

No, God may not always answer as quickly as you'd like. But remember, God not only knows everything, but He also knows what's best for you. So if He hasn't answered you yet, it's for a good reason.

The next time you get worried because God hasn't answered your prayer yet, *stop*. Open up the Bible and read about God and who He really is—loyal, faithful, and strong. Trust that His answer is coming and then let His peace fill your heart.

> *Lord, I know You are good. Help me wait patiently*
> *for Your answer to my prayers, amen.*

TODAY WITH JESUS . . . FOCUS ON HIM.

GOD WILL CATCH YOU

Fig trees may not grow figs. There may be no grapes on the
vines. . . . But I will still be glad in the Lord. I will rejoice
in God my Savior. The Lord God gives me my strength. . . .
He leads me safely on the steep mountains.

HABAKKUK 3:17–19

Have you ever had trouble climbing a steep hill? The path looked solid and trustworthy, so you kept climbing higher and higher. Then—suddenly—you were slipping, sliding, and falling as the dirt and pebbles crumbled from under your feet. You grabbed for anything you could reach to stop your slide—rocks, bits of grass, small trees. It's frightening when the thing you're trusting in lets you down.

That can happen with people too. Someone you trust suddenly changes—and you're left falling and grabbing for anything to hold onto. It's terrifying! But that will *never* happen with God. He won't ever change, and He won't let you fall. He is rock solid all the time.

In fact, when someone lets you down, grab onto God—He won't let go of you. He'll pick you up, dust you off, and walk with you all the way to the top.

Lord, I'm so grateful You're always there to catch
me when others let me down, amen.

TODAY WITH JESUS . . . BELIEVE GOD WILL CATCH YOU.

THE ONE TO TURN TO

Depend on the Lord and his strength. Always go to him for help.
PSALM 105:4

Maybe your yesterday wasn't so great, so you talked to God. He cheered you up by reminding you how much He loves you. And the day before that wasn't so great, either, so you read God's Word to help you remember He always takes care of His children. In fact, maybe the last few days—or even longer—have been pretty rough. So you've been depending on God a lot to get you through.

And you know what? That's *fabulous*! Of course, it's not great you're having a tough time, but it *is* fabulous that you know who to turn to for help: God. He's always the right one to look to for help, love, comfort, strength—for whatever you need. God *wants* you to come to Him.

Others may get tired of listening or helping, but God never will. He'll encourage you every second of every day—because He loves you.

Lord Jesus, thank You for always being
ready to listen and help, amen.

**TODAY WITH JESUS . . . READ PSALM 34:3–8 AND
REMEMBER GOD IS ALWAYS THERE FOR YOU.**

PERFECTLY AMAZING

In Christ Jesus, God made us new people so that we would do
good works. God had planned in advance those good works
for us. He had planned for us to live our lives doing them.

EPHESIANS 2:10

God is so amazing—He knows absolutely everything! Not just everything about today, but also everything about yesterday *and* tomorrow. That means He knows every detail of your life from beginning to end. *And* He has a plan for your life.

The thing about God's plan is this: He won't show you the whole plan all at once. He'll only show you the next step or two to take. Sometimes you might wish He'd hurry the plan up a little—or at least show you more of it. But that's not His way. By leading you one step at a time, God is teaching you to trust His wisdom and care.

When you're struggling to wait on God, remember that He knows everything, He knows what's best, and He knows what He created you to do. So wait for God . . . because His plan is not only perfect, it's completely amazing.

Lord, waiting isn't my favorite thing, but I'll trust
You and wait for You to lead me, amen.

**TODAY WITH JESUS . . . THINK ABOUT THE
GOOD WORKS GOD HAS PLANNED FOR YOU.**

IS GOD YOUR GOD?

Wait for the Lord's help and follow him. He will honor you.
PSALM 37:34

Waiting is hard—especially when you're waiting on something really big and important. Days go by, and you get up every morning wondering, *Will this be the day?*

Don't give up. Remember, God uses times of waiting to teach you to trust Him. But there is a question you need to ask yourself: have you decided you won't love God anymore if He doesn't give you what you want? Because if you have, then you have a very big problem—because that thing you're waiting for has become your god.

So look at your heart, your thoughts, and feelings. Will you still love God if He says no? Is He still the God of your life? Make sure that He is. Ask Him to remove any fake gods and help you know that He is the One and only true God. Then trust Him . . . especially when He asks you to wait.

*Lord, You are my God. There is nothing I want
more than to be close to You, amen.*

PRAISE GOD TODAY

Paul and Silas were praying and singing songs to
God. . . . Suddenly, there was a big earthquake. . . .
Then all the doors of the jail broke open.

ACTS 16:25–26

No matter what's happening around you today, *remember God.* He is your helper and defender. Praise Him and thank Him for His power, wisdom, and love. Because when you stop to praise God, He lifts you above whatever troubles are happening in your life.

Remember Paul and Silas from the Bible? Even though they were innocent, they were still arrested, beaten, and thrown in jail (Acts 16:16–34). But in spite of all their troubles, they remembered God and sang songs of praise to Him. And because they trusted Him—even in jail—God set them free.

When you praise God, you tell Him and everyone listening that you know how wonderful, loving, and powerful He is. So whether you're having a great day, a horrible day, or something in between, decide to praise God. He'll turn your sorrows into joy and make your happy times even happier.

Lord, You are my God! I praise You for Your power
and glory. And I thank You for Your love, amen.

TODAY WITH JESUS . . . SING A SONG OF PRAISE TO HIM.

GOD WORKS THROUGH YOU

We have this treasure from God.
But we are only like clay jars that hold the treasure.
This shows that this great power is from God, not from us.
2 CORINTHIANS 4:7

God works through you. Yes, *you*! No matter how old you are, when you decide to love and follow God, He'll use you to do His work. God has blessed you with wonderful talents—things He created you to do. When you trust Him, He uses you and those talents to reach His goals. And the more you trust Him, the more He'll work through you.

The trouble is that you worry. You see all your mistakes and the things you aren't so good at, and you think, *How could God use someone like me?* But you're thinking about the wrong thing: yourself. Instead, think about God and His mighty power. He's the One who'll make you able to do what He wants you to do (2 Corinthians 3:5). He will trade your weakness for His strength.

So trust and obey God—and watch for the mighty things He does as He works through you.

God, You created me to do good things for Your
kingdom. Thank You for working through me, amen.

TODAY WITH JESUS . . . LOOK FOR WAYS
GOD WORKS THROUGH YOU.

PLANTING SEEDS

The person who plants a little will have a small harvest. But the person who plants a lot will have a big harvest.

2 CORINTHIANS 9:6

Every day you have choices to make—whom to sit with at lunch, what to say to the new kid in class, whether or not to do your homework. As you choose what to do and say, remember these wise words: *whatever you plant, that is what you'll harvest.* For example, if you plant seeds of kindness, you'll harvest friends. But if you plant seeds of laziness by skipping your homework, you'll harvest a bad grade.

Think about the kind of person you want to be, both today and when you grow up. Are the seeds you're planting with your choices going to help you be that person?

If you want to love God, plant seeds of prayer and Bible study. If you want to love those around you, plant seeds of patience, goodness, and kindness. Be careful with the choices you make—each one is a seed you'll harvest one day.

Lord, help me to plant seeds of Your love and goodness wherever I go, amen.

TODAY WITH JESUS . . . PLANT A SEED OF KINDNESS.

GOD'S POINT OF VIEW

"Earthly food spoils and ruins. So . . . work to get the food that stays good always and gives you eternal life. The Son of Man will give you that food."
JOHN 6:27

When you have a problem, it's only natural to think about it—*especially* how to get rid of it. But sometimes God lets problems into your life to shape you into who He wants you to be. For example, you may want a quick fix, but God's letting that problem hang around so He can teach you to be patient and to trust Him.

That's why it's so important for you to try to see your life from God's point of view—and remember that He's working all things together for your good (Romans 8:28). He's more concerned about your eternal soul than about how comfortable you are today.

If you have a problem that won't go away, talk to God. Ask Him to show you how He's using it. He still may not take that trouble away, but He'll give you the strength you need to get through it.

Lord, help me to see my troubles through Your eyes and show me what I need to learn, amen.

TODAY WITH JESUS . . . ASK WHAT YOU CAN LEARN FROM YOUR TROUBLES.

ANYTHING AND EVERYTHING

Praise the Lord, God our Savior, who helps us every day.
PSALM 68:19 NCV

Do you try to handle everything by yourself—the good and the bad? If you do, then you're probably pretty tired. God *never* wanted you to do everything on your own. Instead, He wants to help you. And if you won't let Him, don't be surprised if He gives you a burden too big to carry all on your own. This teaches you to come to Him for help.

Perhaps the real problem is that you're struggling to trust God to take care of you. You *know* He's saved you, but you wonder if He's too busy to bother with your everyday needs or little troubles. Nothing could be less true.

God not only gave His Son for you—He also counts the very hairs on your head. There's nothing too big or small, too ordinary or too unbelievable for Him. He'll help you handle anything and everything that comes your way.

Lord, help me remember that You're
never too busy for me, amen.

TODAY WITH JESUS . . . TELL HIM ALL ABOUT YOUR DAY.

WHEN GOD FEELS FAR AWAY

Take courage! For I believe God. It will be just as he said.
ACTS 27:25 NLT

S ome days you're so close to God you can almost *feel* Him walking beside you. But other days, it's as if He's on the other side of the moon. And you wonder, *Why does God feel so far away?* Perhaps it's because there's some sin you need to confess. But that may not be it. Remember, God is always working to pull you closer to Him. And though He'll never leave you, He may not let you see Him for a time. Why? So that you'll go looking for Him.

That's what happened to Paul. He was a prisoner headed to Rome when his ship was hit by a terrible storm. The storm raged for days, but Paul never gave up on God. He *knew* God was working everything out for his good—and God did rescue him.

So when God seems far away, remember His promise to never leave you. Then declare, "I will believe God."

> *Father, it's hard to be brave when You feel far*
> *away, but I will believe Your promises, amen.*

TODAY WITH JESUS . . . BELIEVE
GOD IS ALWAYS WITH YOU.

IT'S ALREADY DONE

*Abraham believed in the God who brings the dead back
to life and who creates new things out of nothing.*

ROMANS 4:17 NLT

God promises you amazing things—like living in the wonders of heaven with Him forever. But you can't see forever, and heaven may seem very far away. It's much easier to see the troubles and struggles right in front of you today. But understand this truth: *if God has promised it to you, then it's already done.*

That's what Abraham believed. God promised him a son, but years went by with no baby boy. No one would've blamed Abraham for giving up. After all, he was one hundred years old, and his wife was ninety! But Abraham kept believing. He knew that God had already kept His promise—and was just waiting for the perfect time to reveal it to Abraham.

You may not be able to see heaven yet, but God promises it to you. And He's already got a place prepared just for you (John 14:2). So don't worry about what you can or can't see when it comes to God's promises. Trust that with God, it is all ready for you to enjoy in His time.

*Lord, thank You for Your promises to me. I know
those are promises You've already kept, amen.*

**TODAY WITH JESUS . . . THINK ABOUT
YOUR HOME IN HEAVEN.**

DO YOU NEED TO CHANGE?

*If you reject discipline, you only harm yourself; but if you
listen to correction, you grow in understanding.*
PROVERBS 15:32 NLT

When someone blames you, scolds you, or says you're not doing
something right, those words can hurt—*a lot*. It's tempting to
snap back with some not-so-nice words of your own. But God doesn't
want you to get angry or even (Hebrews 12:15). Instead, ask yourself
if there's any truth in what was said. Yes, there'll be times when there
isn't a bit of truth in it. But there'll be other times when you might
find something you need to change.

Ask God—He always knows. Pray these words: "God, examine me
and know my heart. . . . See if there is any bad thing in me" (Psalm
139:23–24). It's not an easy prayer to pray, but God will show you if
there's anything you need to work on. And if there is something you
need to change, do it. If there isn't, then forgive the one who said
those hurtful words.

*Lord, show me what I need to change, and
then please help me to do it, amen.*

**TODAY WITH JESUS . . . CHOOSE TO LISTEN
INSTEAD OF GETTING ANGRY.**

A POWERFUL PRAYER PERSON

When a believing person prays, great things happen.

JAMES 5:16 NCV

When God's children pray, amazing things happen—you're given new strength, you change, others change, people are healed, and sins are forgiven. You know this, yet you may be thinking, *I pray, but I don't see God's power working. Am I doing something wrong?* If you're not seeing God's answers to your prayers, it's time to ask yourself some questions:

- Are you remembering who God is—the King of kings, the Lord of all creation? Or are you treating Him like a magic genie who's just supposed to grant your wishes?
- When you pray, do you believe God will answer?
- Are you ready to accept His answers if they're different from what you want?
- Are you praying, "Your will be done, God, not my will"?

You can be a powerful prayer person. But first you must trust God with your prayers *and* His answers to them.

Father God, help me learn how to pray and to trust You to answer my prayers, amen.

TODAY WITH JESUS . . . BELIEVE GOD WILL ANSWER YOUR PRAYERS.

APRIL 25

JESUS PRAYS FOR YOU

He is always able to save those who come to God
through him. He can do this, because he always lives,
ready to help those who come before God.
HEBREWS 7:25

When you're struggling with a problem, you may feel all alone. You may think no one else truly understands what you're going through. But Jesus understands. And He's praying for you. That's right, *Jesus*—the Lord God Himself—is praying for *you*.

That's what He did for His disciple Peter. Before Jesus went to the cross, He knew the Devil would test Peter, and that Peter would say he didn't know Jesus. So Jesus told Peter, "I have prayed that you will not lose your faith! Help your brothers be stronger when you come back to me" (Luke 22:32). Jesus was saying, "It's going to get tough, but I'm with you. And after you get through this, help others who are hurting."

Jesus does the same for you. When you're struggling, He prays for you. You will get through it, and after it's over, you can help someone else get through their struggles too.

Jesus, thank You for praying for me. I know I
can get through anything with You, amen.

TODAY WITH JESUS . . . REMEMBER
JESUS PRAYS FOR YOU.

GO AHEAD AND SHINE

Those who look to him for help will be radiant with joy;
no shadow of shame will darken their faces.

PSALM 34:5 NLT

Have you ever met someone who just seemed to shine? It's almost as if the love of Jesus just spills out of them. The Holy Spirit is so busy working inside them and through them that they don't even realize they're shining with His light. But everyone around them does.

Now think about this: Have you ever been surprised by someone's praise? Do people see good things in you that you don't see in yourself? Maybe someone mentioned your joyful smile or your giving heart. Or maybe it was your kindness, your loyalty, or your self-control that someone admired.

If so, thank God—because that means He's working through you. You may not realize it, but the people around you do. So go ahead and shine—it's the joy of the Lord shining through you.

Lord Jesus, thank You for shining through me. Help
me always to show Your light to the world, amen.

TODAY WITH JESUS . . . SHINE WITH JESUS' LOVE.

GREATER THAN YOU CAN IMAGINE

No one has ever imagined what God has
prepared for those who love him.
1 CORINTHIANS 2:9

I s there something you want more than anything else? Maybe it's a new game, a bike, or your own room. Or maybe it's to be popular or the star of the team. There's nothing wrong with wanting those things—or thinking about them. But don't let them take over your thoughts. Because if you do, you'll start focusing on yourself and how *you* can get what you want, instead of trusting God to give you what you need. And that will lead you straight to sin.

The good news is no matter how great your imagination is, God's is even greater. And no matter how wonderful your plans, God's are even better (Ephesians 3:20).

So if you're frustrated because you're not getting what you want, and you're tempted to just go after it yourself—stop! Remember the awesomeness of God and His power. Trust Him to create something greater than you could ever imagine.

Lord, please help me to focus on You and
not the things I want, amen.

TODAY WITH JESUS . . . TRUST GOD'S PLANS FOR YOU.

GET READY TO BE BLESSED

For the LORD God is our sun and our shield. He gives us grace and glory.
The LORD will withhold no good thing from those who do what is right.

PSALM 84:11 NLT

Sometimes God asks you to wait for His blessings. But while you're waiting, you may start to worry. You might think, *I've done something wrong—that's why it's taking so long.* Or *God doesn't think I'm good enough for His blessings.*

That's not true! If God is asking you to wait, it's for a reason. Perhaps you need to grow up a bit so you can fully enjoy the blessing. Or perhaps your blessing needs time to develop. Or perhaps the thing you're hoping and praying for wouldn't end up being a blessing to you at all. God wants only the best for you. That means sometimes He's your shield—protecting you from things that would hurt you. And sometimes He shapes and teaches you.

If you're waiting on God's blessings, don't give up. He won't hold back anything that's truly good for you. Trust Him, and get ready to be blessed.

Lord, while I wait for Your blessings, help
me to get ready for them, amen.

TODAY WITH JESUS . . . WAIT FOR GOD'S BLESSINGS.

FIGHT TEMPTATION

Who will save me . . . ? God will. I thank him for
saving me through Jesus Christ our Lord!
ROMANS 7:24–25

You know you shouldn't tell that lie, say those words, cheat on that test, scream at your brother. You know you shouldn't . . . but it's just so *tempting*. Have you figured out that you can't beat temptation on you own? You need help. You need Jesus and His Word.

Sin starts in your thoughts. You think about it, and then you see how it could get you what you want. You want to be popular, so a little juicy gossip will get you noticed. You want good grades, and a little cheat sheet will help. You *think* those things, and the next thing you know, you're doing them.

Let Jesus' truth fight those tempting thoughts. You don't need popularity to be loved or good grades to be important. Here's the truth: you're God's child—perfectly loved and so very important to Him. Fight temptation with His truth—and win.

Lord, help me fight temptation with Your beautiful truth, amen.

TODAY WITH JESUS . . . REMEMBER
YOU ARE A CHILD OF GOD.

ALL FIGURED OUT

Trust the Lord with all your heart. Don't
depend on your own understanding.

PROVERBS 3:5

Have you ever tackled a really tough math problem on your own? You thought you had it all figured out. But then, when the teacher checked it, you realized you were *completely* wrong. You were depending on your own understanding, but your teacher had the real knowledge of how to solve the problem.

The same thing can happen with you and God. You might struggle with a really tough problem. You might even think you have it all figured out, but then things don't turn out the way you expect. That's because only God knows all the facts. You can see some things, but only God can see everything—including the past and the future. So don't depend on yourself; depend on God. Ask Him to show you what He wants you to do. His answer may not always make sense at the time, but it will always be perfectly right for you.

Lord, when I think I've figured things out on my own,
remind me to look for You and follow You instead, amen.

TODAY WITH JESUS . . . TRUST GOD
WITH ALL YOUR HEART.

MAY

PRAY WITHOUT WORRY

"Surely your heavenly Father will give good things to those who ask him."
MATTHEW 7:11

When you pray, do you ever wonder, *Am I asking God for the right things? How do I know if what I'm asking will please Him?*

You don't have to worry about those things. First, remember that when you become a child of God, He sends His Holy Spirit to live inside you. The Spirit will work to help you do what pleases God (Philippians 2:13). Not only will He help you pray, but He'll show you what to pray for (Romans 8:26–27).

And second, God *wants* you to know what pleases Him—He doesn't keep it a secret. He spells it out in the Bible: love Him and love your neighbor (Matthew 22:37–39). When you're truly trying to worship and please God, He'll show you the best way to do it (Psalm 25:12). So don't worry when you pray . . . just pray.

Dear God, thank You for the Holy Spirit and for helping me learn to please You with my prayers, amen.

TODAY WITH JESUS . . . PRAY WITHOUT WORRY.

KNOW GOD

Seek the LORD your God with all your heart and soul.

1 CHRONICLES 22:19 NLT

Never forget how very important you are to God—*or* how important He wants to be to you. God created you to know Him, to have a loving relationship with Him, and to tell others about Him. Yes, it's good to know the facts of the Bible, and it's good to memorize verses. But until you truly know God—as your Savior, protector, and friend, as well as your Lord—you won't understand just how much He loves you or how wonderful His plans for you are.

Ask yourself: When you read the Bible, are you looking for facts? Or are you trying to get to know God? When you pray, are you only hoping for blessings? Or are you sharing your life with the One who created you?

God doesn't just want you to know *about Him*—He wants you to know *Him*.

Lord, I do want to know You, not just about You. Please use Your Word to show me who You are, amen.

TODAY WITH JESUS . . . GET TO KNOW GOD.

SEEING THROUGH GOD'S EYES

You are the giver of life. Your light lets us enjoy life.
PSALM 36:9

When you decide to put God first in your thoughts, you'll see the world and your life in a whole new way. Things that worry you don't seem so big. Troubles that make you feel weak and helpless seem less troublesome when you put them next to God's strength. The way you see your friends, family, enemies, and even yourself changes because you see everyone through the eyes of God's love.

This change won't happen overnight, though. It takes time—time spent talking and listening to God and studying His Word. But over time, you'll see that He's able to help with anything you face. There's no need for worry or fear because there's nothing that can defeat God. He loves you, protects you, and takes care of you. He'll light up the darkest of times and bring joy to your sadness. Spend time with God—and let Him show you the world through His eyes.

Father, show me how You see this world and
who You want me to be in it, amen.

**TODAY WITH JESUS . . . PUT GOD
FIRST IN YOUR THOUGHTS.**

DO WHAT GOD SAYS

*"Obey me, and I will be your God and you will be my people.
Do all that I command, and good things will happen to you."*

No matter what you face today, *obey God*. Then leave whatever happens next up to Him—knowing that you've done the right thing.

If there's an argument between two of your friends, try to make peace (2 Timothy 2:24–26). If a problem is worrying you, talk to God about it (Isaiah 41:10). If someone wrongs you, don't get even—forgive them (Ephesians 4:32), and trust God to make everything right (Isaiah 54:17). If someone is hurting, offer comfort (2 Corinthians 1:3–4). And tell others about Jesus whenever you can (John 3:16).

If you're not sure what to do, pray (Psalm 32:8). If you're tempted to do something you know is wrong, run away from it (1 Corinthians 10:13). Do *everything* as if you were doing it for God (Colossians 3:23). You can't go wrong if you obey God. So trust Him—even when it's tough—and He'll bless you for it.

*Lord, I want to obey You in everything I do. Please show me
what to do—and then give me the courage to do it, amen.*

TODAY WITH JESUS . . . DO WHAT GOD SAYS.

ALWAYS WITH YOU

"You can be sure that I will be with you always."
MATTHEW 28:20

Do you know that God is with you—right this very second? It's true. You may not always feel Him with you, but He's there. He never, ever leaves you. When you're hurting or stressed out or worried, it may *seem* that God is far away. But the fact is, when you decide to follow Him, He sends His Holy Spirit to live inside you—that's how God is *always* with you (Ephesians 1:13–14). As a child of God, you won't ever be without Him.

That is an awesome truth! The all-powerful God who created absolutely everything is right there with you. You never have to worry or be afraid because He never leaves you to fight your battles alone or figure out your troubles on your own. His perfect strength, unlimited wisdom, and never-failing love are always yours—even when you don't feel them.

Look for God today—He's there!

> *Dear Lord, please open my eyes and show*
> *me Your presence in my life, amen.*

TODAY WITH JESUS . . . LOOK FOR GOD.

THINGS *WILL* CHANGE

Our hope is in the Lord. He is our help, our shield to protect us.

PSALM 33:20

Does it ever seem like things will never change? Maybe there's a problem that sticks around so long that you start to think it will never go away, or that thing you're dealing with will never get better. It's as if God doesn't even hear your prayers. And like King David did, you just want to say to God, "How long will you forget me, Lord? . . . Forever?" (Psalm 13:1).

Dearest one, God hasn't forgotten you, and He does hear your prayers. He's simply asking you to wait until His perfect answer comes. And He won't make you wait any longer than you can handle--if you lean on Him.

Turn to God. Pray. Read His Word. And if you think you can't stand one second more, tell Him. He'll give you His strength to get you through. He is working. Trust Him to change things for your good.

Lord, I will trust You. Even when I don't see You
working in my life, I'll believe that You are, amen.

TODAY WITH JESUS . . . BELIEVE GOD IS WORKING.

NO STORM WILL SINK YOU

"The words I say . . . will not return to me empty. . . .
They succeed in doing what I send them to do."
ISAIAH 55:11

When a storm blows in, the ship's captain drops an anchor. That holds the boat safely in place until the storm passes. In life God's Word is your anchor. And when storms blow into your life—like a best friend moving away, parents fighting, or even losing someone you love—God's Word keeps you safely anchored close to Him.

How? By believing the promises that God's Word gives you—*even* when the world says it's impossible. Remember Peter? When the storm blew in, Jesus called to him to walk out on the water. Impossible, right? But not with Jesus! Peter *did* step out of the boat, and he *did* walk on water—at least until he looked at how big the storm was and stopped believing that Jesus was bigger (Matthew 14:25–33). That's when he started sinking.

But you don't have to sink when the storms hit. Instead, believe God. Believe His promises. Believe He's bigger than any storm. And no storm will ever sink you.

Jesus, help me believe Your Word—no matter
how big the storm seems to be, amen.

**TODAY WITH JESUS . . . BELIEVE HE'S
BIGGER THAN ANY STORM.**

DEAL WITH IT

"When the Spirit of truth comes he will lead you into all truth."
JOHN 16:13

When you're praying, do you ever start to feel sad or upset? Do you suddenly remember something you need to tell God or some sin you need to confess? If so, it may be that the Holy Spirit is bringing those things into your thoughts so that you'll deal with them.

For example, if you're praying for someone, but then remember a time she hurt you, and your thoughts turn angry—then God may be telling you that you need to forgive her. Or perhaps you're praying for a teammate who is sick, but then start thinking about how you'll get more playing time while he's out. That's God pointing out your selfishness and jealousy so that you can confess those sins to Him.

The Lord wants to heal *all* your hurts and take away *all* your sins—even the ones you've forgotten are there. So when He brings something into your thoughts, deal with it.

Lord, please show me my sins—even the ones
I've forgotten. And please forgive me, amen.

TODAY WITH JESUS . . . LISTEN WHILE YOU PRAY.

A WALKING, TALKING BILLBOARD

"He who believes in me will do the same things that I do. He will do even greater things than these."
JOHN 14:12

When you're a kid, there's so much you can't do yet. You can't take food to someone who's sick, because you can't really cook—or drive! Maybe you're not old enough to get a job or buy your own clothes or food, so you certainly can't help others do those things. You may wonder, *How can God possibly use me?*

But God *can* use you—and He will if you'll let Him. Remember, when you accept Jesus as your Savior, His Holy Spirit comes to live inside you *and* work through you. You become a walking, talking billboard for God's amazing power, wisdom, and love. You don't have to cook or drive or get a job to be useful. Simply let God use you to show other people His love.

You see, the question isn't, *Can God use me?* It's, *Will I let Him?* Just be ready for God to work through you—and He'll take care of the rest.

Lord, use me to tell others about how amazing You are, amen.

TODAY WITH JESUS . . . LET GOD USE YOU.

WHEN PRAISE SEEMS IMPOSSIBLE

I will call to the Lord. He is worthy of praise.

PSALM 18:3

There will be days when it's tough to praise the Lord. Sometimes your heart and your head may be filled with worry, or you're just dealing with some tough situations. On those days, thanking Jesus may seem almost impossible.

But even in the middle of your very worst times, you still have reasons to praise and thank Jesus. Just think about it: He died to take away your sins and give you life forever in heaven (John 3:16). He has already defeated every trouble you'll ever face—even if you don't see the victory yet. He loves you with a love that will never end (Jeremiah 31:3), and He'll never, ever leave you (Hebrews 13:5).

When you think about who Jesus really is and all He's done for you, how could you *not* thank Him? Think about Him—instead of yourself—and all He's done for you, and praise will be no problem.

Jesus, You are so good and so wonderful. You deserve all my thanks and praise, amen.

**TODAY WITH JESUS . . . PRAISE
JESUS FOR ALL HE'S DONE.**

GOD . . . YOUR DEFENDER

Our fight is not against people on earth. We are
fighting against . . . the spiritual powers of evil.
EPHESIANS 6:12

Do you ever feel like you're in the middle of a war zone? Friendships blow up, parents are fighting, and there's stress everywhere you turn. Even the simplest things become difficult: You take out the trash, but the bag rips and spills yucky stuff everywhere. You try to share a joke with your sister, but she thinks you're laughing at her. Tempers get hot and everyone seems grouchy. And soon, you're feeling beaten down and worthless.

That, dear friend, is a spiritual battle. The Devil is trying to pull you away from trusting in God by throwing every trouble he can think of at you. If he can keep you thinking about yourself and your troubles—instead of God and serving Him—then the Devil wins. Don't fall for his trap!

Defeat the Devil by shouting, "I trust God!" Remember you are God's child, and He's stronger than the Devil. Trust Him to defend you.

Father, I will trust You. Thank You for defending
me against the Devil's attacks, amen.

**TODAY WITH JESUS . . . REMEMBER GOD
HAS ALREADY BEATEN THE DEVIL.**

FORGIVE

If someone does wrong to you, then forgive him. Forgive each other because the Lord forgave you.

COLOSSIANS 3:13

Is there someone you need to forgive? Perhaps, even as you're reading this, God's Holy Spirit is whispering that person's name into your thoughts. It might even be someone you thought you'd forgiven, but now you realize that you haven't completely let go of your anger.

When you refuse to forgive others, it actually hurts you most. It damages your health, steals your peace, chases away your joy, and hurts your relationships with others. An unforgiving heart can lock you up in a prison of bitterness and anger—and that's not how God wants you to live.

God knows everything that happened, and He'll take care of it in His own perfect way. Stop worrying about getting even, and just forgive. Give your anger and hurt to God. Let Him heal you and set you free.

Lord, please help me forgive _____. Please take away my hurt and anger, amen.

TODAY WITH JESUS . . . FORGIVE THOSE WHO HAVE WRONGED YOU.

BE PATIENT

Let us hold firmly to the hope that we have confessed.
We can trust God to do what he promised.
HEBREWS 10:23

When you have a problem, it's tempting to rush out and try to fix it on your own. Instead, be patient, talk to God, and trust Him to show you the right way to go.

Think about Queen Esther. When she found out her people were going to be attacked, it must have been so tempting to run straight to King Xerxes for help. After all, he could stop the attack. But Esther knew that rushing out and trying to fix everything herself would be a mistake. Instead, she asked all the Jewish people to fast with her for three days. This gave them time to think and pray. *Then* Esther went to the king, and God used her to save her people (Esther 3–7).

When problems come your way, be patient. Take time to talk to God and then wait for Him to show you the way to go. Remember, God promises to take care of you—and He always keeps His promises.

Lord, it's so hard to be patient, but I trust that You know
what's best. I'll wait on You to show me the way to go, amen.

TODAY WITH JESUS . . . TRUST HIM
TO SHOW YOU THE WAY.

PUT GOD FIRST

*"Seek first God's kingdom and what God wants. Then
all your other needs will be met as well."*

MATTHEW 6:33 NCV

What do you want most? Is it the latest game or gadget? Is it to be popular or make the team? Or is it God?

It's okay to love the people of this world. And it's okay to want the things of this world. The problem comes when you love others or want things *more* than God. If your days are full of doubts, anger, jealousy, fears, sadness, or worry, then it may be that God has slipped away from the center of your life. Think about it: Are you putting friendships or sports before time with God? Do you have time to play on the Internet, but not to read God's Word?

Talk to God about it. Ask Him to show you anything that's becoming more important to you than Him. If you put God first and do the things He wants, then He'll bless all the rest of your life.

*Lord, if there is anything that I'm putting ahead of You,
please show me. Help me keep You first in my life, amen.*

TODAY WITH JESUS . . . PUT HIM FIRST.

A HUGE SUCCESS

The world is passing away.
And everything that people want in the world is passing away.
But the person who does what God wants lives forever.
1 JOHN 2:17

What is your definition of success? Is it being popular or powerful? Is it having lots of money, or being beautiful or famous? That's how the world usually thinks of success. But God sees success as something very different.

First of all, you don't have to prove yourself to God—He already thinks you're important. You're *so* loved and *so* valuable to Him that He sent His own Son to save you. For God, success isn't about fame or fortune; it's about loving Him and becoming all He created you to be.

Don't chase after the treasures of this world, because they never last for long anyway. Instead, chase after God's treasures—things like love, joy, peace, patience, kindness, goodness, faithfulness, gentleness, and self-control (Galatians 5:22–23). Because when you choose to fill your life with the things that please God, you'll always be a huge success.

Jesus, help me do the things that make You happy, amen.

TODAY WITH JESUS . . . BE A HUGE SUCCESS TO GOD.

STUCK IN THE MIDDLE

Don't be afraid! Stand still and see the Lord save you today.

EXODUS 14:13

Have you ever been stuck in the middle of something you have absolutely no control over? Maybe it's something small like a fight between friends—or something huge like a sickness or moving to another town. You may wonder, *God, why have You let this happen?*

That's exactly how the Israelites felt after they left Egypt. They were stuck right in the middle—trapped between the Red Sea on one side and the Egyptian army on the other. They probably wondered where God was. But God hadn't left them. Instead, He let them get "stuck in the middle" so He could show them His power to save them. As His people watched in awe, God parted the deep waters of the Red Sea, and the people escaped through it on dry ground.

When you're "stuck in the middle," remember that God is with you. Watch for His great power as He works to rescue you.

Lord, when I'm "stuck in the middle," I'll trust
You to make a way out for me, amen.

TODAY WITH JESUS . . . THANK HIM
FOR HIS GREAT POWER.

MAY 17

A GOD WHO LOVES

*We have freedom now because Christ made us free. So stand
strong. Do not change and go back into the slavery of the law.*
GALATIANS 5:1

God loves you *unconditionally*. That means there's nothing you can
do to stop Him from loving you. He doesn't love you more when
you do everything right, and He doesn't love you less when you mess
up. God loves you because that's who *He* is—a God who loves.

Think about this as you go through your day: If things go wrong,
you may wonder if God is punishing you. But remember, Jesus already
took care of your punishment on the cross (Romans 6:23). God may
discipline—or teach—you to help you stop sinning (Hebrews 12:5–11),
but if you follow Jesus, He'll never declare you guilty of your sins
again (Romans 6:23).

God loves you simply because you're you—you don't have to earn
His love by being "good enough." You just have to accept God's love
and then praise Him for it by obeying Him as best you can.

*God, thank You for loving me just as I am. Help me
show You my love by living the right way, amen.*

SAFE THROUGH EVERY STORM

He calmed the storm to a whisper. . . . He
brought them safely into harbor!
PSALM 107:29–30 NLT

God puts dreams and goals in your heart. Sometimes they're for right now, but sometimes they're for far away in the future. Don't worry, though. God knows just what you need to get you to those far-away goals and dreams. He has a path all laid out for you—and He'll help you follow it, one step at a time. Now, that path might look different from the one you would've picked for yourself, but you can believe God has made it the perfect path for you.

Some people turn away from God's path because they're afraid. Maybe they see a huge obstacle to climb over or a storm of trouble blocking the way. If that happens to you, don't give up. Trust God and keep following Him. Climbing over that obstacle will build up your muscles of faith and make you stronger. And you'll learn to trust God as He keeps you safe through every storm.

Lord, I know You have planned the perfect path for
me. Help me to keep following You, amen.

TODAY WITH JESUS . . . FOLLOW GOD'S PATH.

WAIT FOR GOD

Wait and trust the Lord. . . . Don't be upset; it only leads to trouble.
PSALM 37:7–8

If you know what God wants you to do, but you don't do it—that's *not* a good thing. And sometimes the hardest thing God asks you to do is to *wait.*

King Saul learned that lesson the hard way. The enemy army was about to attack, and Saul and his men were terrified. Saul knew God had told the prophet Samuel to offer sacrifices before the battle, but Samuel hadn't gotten there yet and the enemy was getting restless. Saul knew he couldn't defeat the enemy without God's help, and he was frightened and tired of waiting for Samuel. So Saul disobeyed God and offered the sacrifice himself. And because Saul didn't obey God, the Lord took his kingdom away from him (1 Samuel 13:1–14).

Don't make the same mistake. Don't let fear make you do something you know you shouldn't. Wait for God, and follow Him. He'll show you what to do and bless you when you do it.

Father, help me know what You want me
to do—and help me do it, amen.

TODAY WITH JESUS . . . WAIT WHEN GOD SAYS WAIT.

SEEDS OF TIME

*We must not become tired of doing good. We will receive our
harvest of eternal life at the right time. We must not give up!*

GALATIANS 6:9

You pray, you read the Bible, and you wait and listen for God to
guide you—but when you look around at your troubles, you may
sometimes wonder if it really matters. *Yes!* It does matter. Praying,
reading His Word, and listening for His voice pulls you closer to God
and lets Him work more and more in your life.

You may not see it right away, but God *is* working. It's like planting a tiny seed. You can't see all that it will grow into when you plant
it. But one day, you will see it bloom. Time spent with God is the same
way. You may not see what you're planting right now. But one day, your
life will bloom with love, joy, peace, patience, kindness, goodness,
faithfulness, gentleness, and self-control.

Don't give up. Keep planting seeds of time with God—and your
life will be filled with His beautiful blooms.

*Lord, I pray that Your love and Your Spirit will bloom
in my life for all the world to see, amen.*

**TODAY WITH JESUS . . . PLANT
SEEDS OF TIME WITH GOD.**

LESSON LEARNED

God knows the way that I take. When he has
tested me, I will come out pure as gold.
JOB 23:10

If you keep facing the same kind of problem over and over again, it means the Lord is trying to teach you something. Maybe you need to learn to be more giving, kind, or patient. Or perhaps you need to be more careful with your words and attitudes. Whatever it is God wants to teach you, He'll keep giving you chances to learn it. Why? Because He wants you to be more like Jesus.

No, God's lessons aren't always fun. In fact, they can be quite painful. But so often, it's only when you're hurting or don't know what to do that you completely lean on God to help you—and that is when He can best teach you.

Is there a problem in your life that just keeps popping up? Ask yourself, *What could God be trying to teach me?* Then trust Him, follow Him, and learn the lesson He wants to teach you.

Dear God, please help me learn the lessons
You want to teach me, amen.

TODAY WITH JESUS . . . LEARN FROM YOUR PROBLEMS.

ONE HUNDRED PERCENT

I know the one in whom I trust, and I am sure that he is able to guard what I have entrusted to him until the day of his return.

2 TIMOTHY 1:12 NLT

Trust God. Believe with every bit of your being that He will keep every single one of His promises. Don't just say, "I hope God will help me," or, "I know He *can* make everything work out." Show God how much you trust Him by boldly declaring, "I am one-hundred-percent positive that my Father God *will* help me. It's already as good as done."

When you *know* God will keep His promises, you don't have to worry. You know that you can handle whatever comes your way because God is with you and He is able to take care of you. Nothing is impossible for Him!

So thank God for answering your prayers—even if you don't see His answers yet. Trust Him completely. He *will* keep His promises, and He *will* take care of you. You can be one-hundred-percent sure of that.

Lord, I know—without a doubt—You will help me. Thank You for always being there for me, amen.

TODAY WITH JESUS . . . TRUST GOD ONE HUNDRED PERCENT.

THE WAY YOU LIVE

Live the kind of life that honors and pleases the Lord in every way.
COLOSSIANS 1:10

Y ou are important. It doesn't matter how big you are, or how old you are, or what you can or can't do yet. God created you with His love and with His wisdom for a reason—and a huge part of that reason is telling others about Him. And because His Holy Spirit lives inside you, the things you say and do can help other people learn about Jesus.

Whether you see it or not, the way you live sends other people a message about God. So ask yourself: when your friends see you struggling with a problem, do they see you turning to God for help? When they see the way you treat others, do they see His love and kindness? When they see you deciding between doing right and doing wrong, do they see you choosing to obey God?

Show God how much you love Him by living a life that helps others learn about Him.

Lord, help me live a life that shows other
people how wonderful You are, amen.

TODAY WITH JESUS . . . SHOW OTHERS HIS LOVE.

GIVE YOUR DAY TO GOD

"I leave you peace. My peace I give you. I do not give it to you as the world does. So don't let your hearts be troubled. Don't be afraid."

JOHN 14:27

When you focus on what *you* can do, instead of what *God* can do, your life will feel like one problem after another. But when you focus on God and what He can do in your life, He'll help you overcome those problems and your life will be filled with His victory, peace, and joy.

If you're worried or upset right now, could it be because you're trusting in yourself to get through the day instead of trusting God to help you?

Every day you have a choice to make: either try to struggle through your day all on your own—or trust God to help you. He's the only One who can take away your worries and give you peace. And He's the only One who can truly defeat all the troubles of this world. So give your day to God, and let Him fill your day with His blessings.

Lord God, help me to focus on all that You can do instead of all that I can't do, amen.

TODAY WITH JESUS . . . CHOOSE TO TRUST GOD WITH YOUR DAY.

HOW CAN YOU BE SURE?

"My people will know who I am. They will know I am God.
And they will know that I am the one speaking to them."
ISAIAH 52:6

You've prayed about it. You've read God's Word. You talked it over with someone you trust. And you think you know what God wants you to do, but how can you be sure? That's when it's time to pray some more. And as you pray, ask these questions:

- Lord, does this choice match what the Bible says? Please show me in Your Word.
- Jesus, does this fit with Your plan for my life?
- God, if this is the right choice, please fill my heart with peace.
- Father, if I choose this way, will I be obeying you? Will I be giving You glory?

Listen carefully to the Lord as you pray and as you go through your day. Keep praying and set your heart to please Him—and He will certainly answer you.

Father, I want to please You with my life. Please
show me what You want me to do, amen.

ROCK BOTTOM

He lifted me out of the pit of destruction, out of
the sticky mud. He stood me on a rock.

PSALM 40:2

Have you heard the phrase "rock bottom"? It means things can't get any worse. Sometimes God lets you hit rock bottom. Why? Because you can be so stubborn about doing things your own way, that's the only way God can get your attention. But don't give up. God won't leave you at rock bottom. Instead, He'll use that time to teach you, and then He'll lift you up again.

That's what happened to the people of Judah long ago. They thought their land, history, and inheritance gave them worth. But when the Babylonians captured them, they lost everything. They hit rock bottom. That's when they realized God was more important than all those other things—that He was the One who gave them value and made them successful. When they learned that lesson (and it took a long time!), God rescued them and returned them to their land.

When you hit rock bottom, remember that God is all that truly matters. Trust Him to rescue you.

Lord, help me always to remember that You are
the most important thing in my life, amen.

TODAY WITH JESUS . . . THANK GOD
FOR ALL HE HAS DONE.

A SHINING LIGHT

*God did not give us a spirit that makes us afraid. He
gave us a spirit of power and love and self-control.*
2 TIMOTHY 1:7

When you get slammed by hard times, it can be hard to remember how good God is and just how much He loves you. The apostle Paul knew that Timothy was getting slammed by troubles. Believers were being persecuted. False teachers were telling lies about Jesus and causing trouble in Timothy's church. Paul was worried about his friend.

So Paul taught Timothy how to stay strong—advice that will work for you too (2 Timothy 1:3–14). First, admit you're having troubles. Second, stay close to God—even if He feels far away. Do that by praying, reading His Word, letting other believers encourage you, and obeying God. And third, ask God to forgive you of any sins.

These things remind you of how good God is and how much He loves you. When you choose to stay close to God even in hard times, He'll make you a shining light in this dark world.

*Lord, remind me each day of Your goodness
and the greatness of Your love, amen.*

YOU HAVEN'T BEEN FORGOTTEN

"Did I not I tell you that if you believe, you will see the glory of God?"

JOHN 11:40 NIV

You need help, so you turn to God. You pray and read His Word and try to listen for Him—but sometimes He still doesn't seem to answer. And you wonder, *Has God forgotten me?*

Mary and Martha wondered that same thing. Their brother, Lazarus, was dying, so they sent for Jesus. *He* could heal their brother. But when Jesus didn't come, Lazarus died. Why didn't Jesus come? Was it because He'd forgotten them or didn't love them? Of course not! Jesus loved them very much. And when He *did* come, He raised Lazarus from the dead—showing the glorious power of God and causing many more people to believe in Him. Lazarus's death was all part of His amazing plan (John 11:1–45).

If God doesn't seem to be answering you, don't worry—He hasn't forgotten you. Instead, be on the lookout for the amazing way He's going to use your troubles as part of His plan.

Jesus, I know You answer every prayer. So even if I don't see the answer right now, I will trust You, amen.

TODAY WITH JESUS . . . BELIEVE HE WILL ANSWER YOU.

THINKING ABOUT GOD

I discipline my body like an athlete, training it to do what it should.
1 CORINTHIANS 9:27 NLT

Self-control means . . . well . . . controlling yourself. It's making yourself do what you know you should, whether it's exercising, eating right, or not throwing a fit if you don't get your way. You also need self-control when you pray because it's so easy to get distracted.

If you're having trouble keeping your thoughts fixed on God, turn to the book of Psalms and start reading. Ask God to open up His Word to you. Pray, "Father God, show me what these words mean. Use them to help me know who You really are."

Then keep reading until the Lord speaks to you. Now, you probably won't hear a big, booming voice like Moses heard at the burning bush. Instead, it'll be the soft whisper of a thought about who God is and who He wants you to be. But to hear it, you'll need to listen closely—and that takes self-control.

Father, help me control my thoughts and
keep them fixed on You, amen.

TODAY WITH JESUS . . . PICK A CHAPTER
TO READ FROM PSALMS.

BE THANKFUL!

I will praise you, Lord, with all my heart.

PSALM 9:1

If you want a life filled with joy, you need a heart filled with thankfulness. Look for the good in every situation—sometimes you'll have to look hard—and choose to be thankful no matter what's happening.

"But how?" you ask. How can you be thankful even when bad things are happening? Start by counting your blessings. Because even on your worst days, your life is filled with blessings. Think about Jesus and all He's done to forgive and save you. Remember how wonderful God is—He never leaves you or forgets you. He loves, protects, and takes care of you always. And don't forget to be thankful for the Holy Spirit, who guides you and helps you live in a way that pleases God.

No matter what's happening today, you have so much to be thankful for. So praise God for your blessings—and He'll fill your life with joy.

Lord, thank You so much for loving me and
for all that You do for me, amen.

TODAY WITH JESUS . . . SING A SONG OF PRAISE TO GOD.

SOARING LIKE AN EAGLE

*Those who trust in the L*ORD *will find new strength.*
They will soar high on wings like eagles.
ISAIAH 40:31 NLT

Doing the right thing can be hard, especially when the world so often tells you it's okay to do wrong. When you get tired of the battle—of the fight to do right—what should you do? Should you just give in and do whatever the world says? No! Turn to God for help.

If you trust God—keeping your eyes on Him and not the world—then God will give you new strength so that you can soar up high like an eagle.

Even when an eagle is flying high in the sky, it can lock its eyes on a fish far below. Then, no matter how hard the wind blows, it can swoop in and snatch up its prize. In a way, that's your goal too—to lock your eyes on God. He'll give you the strength to keep flying until you can claim your prize in heaven.

Lord, when I'm tired of trying to do what's right, please give
me the strength to keep my eyes locked on You, amen.

TODAY WITH JESUS . . . ASK HIM TO
HELP YOU DO WHAT'S RIGHT.

JUNE

WORKING FOR GOD

In all the work you are doing, work . . . as if you
were working for the Lord, not for men
COLOSSIANS 3:23

Finish your homework. Wash the dishes. Take out the trash. Feed the cat. The daily stuff of life isn't always fun. But the fact is, all through your life, you're going to be asked to do things you don't particularly want to do. Maybe you think you're too busy or those things are "beneath" you. You might have a bad attitude when it comes to things like homework and chores. *Don't.* Because even though you probably don't think of those things as ways to serve God, they are.

Your attitude toward the daily "stuff" of life is so very important. Why? Because one day, God will ask if you honored Him in *everything* you did—yes, even taking out the trash. Tackle everything as if you were doing it for God Himself . . . because you are. And one day He'll reward you.

> *Lord, help me to do the things I need to do with a*
> *smile—because I'm working for You, amen.*

TODAY WITH JESUS . . . DO EVERYTHING FOR HIM.

STOP, LOOK, AND LISTEN

I wait quietly before God, for my victory comes from him.

PSALM 62:1 NLT

You've probably heard the saying, "Stop, look, and listen before you cross the street." It's good advice, and it will help keep you safe. But "stop, look, and listen" is good advice for more than just crossing a street. It's so easy to get in a hurry and rush through your day—and not even notice all the blessings God has placed all around your world. So *stop* and notice the beautiful trees and flowers, puppies and kittens, rainbows and blue skies. *Look* around at all that God has given you—family, friends, a home. And take time to *listen* to the sounds of creation, to a friend, or to someone who needs a friend.

And don't make the mistake of rushing through your time with God. *Stop* and simply sit with Him for a moment. *Look* in His Word. And *listen* for Him to guide you and show you the way to go.

Lord, today I will stop, look, and listen for You and for all the blessings You've placed in my life, amen.

TODAY WITH JESUS . . . STOP, LOOK, AND LISTEN FOR HIM.

MOUNTAIN CLIMBING

*Every valley should be raised up. Every mountain and hill should
be made flat. . . . Then the glory of the Lord will be shown.*
ISAIAH 40:4–5

There are two kinds of mountains. The first kind soars up out of
the ground. When you're at the bottom of that kind of mountain,
you have two choices: stay at the bottom *or* start climbing.

The second kind of mountain is a problem or a challenge so
big that it soars up and over your life. When you're at the bottom of
that kind of mountain, you also have two choices: stay at the bottom
because you're too worried and scared to do anything else *or* start
climbing because you know Jesus will help you.

Whatever mountain you're facing, remember this: the secret to
mountain climbing—the rocky kind or the problem kind—is not to
look at how big the mountain is; instead, look at how big your God is.
No mountain is a match for Him (Matthew 21:21). Trust God to get you
to the top . . . one step at a time.

*Lord, You are the master of mountains. I'll
trust You to get me to the top, amen.*

**TODAY WITH JESUS . . . LOOK AT
HIM, NOT THE MOUNTAIN.**

YOUR HOME IN HEAVEN

You have been saved by grace because you believe. You did not save yourselves. It was a gift from God.

EPHESIANS 2:8

Have you ever felt like God was mad at you? Maybe it's because absolutely everything around you is going wrong, and so you start to wonder, *Does God still love me? Am I still going to heaven?*

Sweet child, those kinds of thoughts and worries were planted in your mind by the Devil himself. He wants you to worry. He wants you to think God is angry with you. He wants you to question whether you'll go to heaven. But the Devil is a liar. Don't listen to him!

Here's the truth: God *never* stops loving you. Your home in heaven was bought and paid for by Jesus' own blood on the cross. And nothing—*absolutely nothing*—the Devil says or does can take that away from you. When you are God's child, your home in heaven is completely safe and certain. Don't ever let the Devil tell you anything different.

Lord Jesus, thank You for loving me and for saving me. You are so good to me, amen.

TODAY WITH JESUS . . . THANK HIM FOR YOUR HOME IN HEAVEN.

A JOB TO DO

Be sure to do the work the Lord gave you.
COLOSSIANS 4:17

You have a job to do. Yes, there are chores your parents give you and homework your teachers assign you. But God also has a job for you to do. The question is: are you doing it?

You see, when God created you, He gave you special gifts and talents. And God expects you to use those talents to serve Him and tell others about Him. If you have a gift for singing, are you singing praises to God? If you have a gift for storytelling or teaching, are you using it to tell others about Jesus? If you have a gift for working with your hands, are you building and creating for God?

God created you to do good things for His kingdom (Ephesians 2:10), and He gave you all the gifts and talents you'll need to do them . . . so go out and serve God with confidence.

Lord, show me the job You want me to do,
and then, please, help me do it, amen.

TODAY WITH JESUS . . . DO WHAT GOD ASKS.

WITH ALL YOUR HEART

*"You will search for me. And when you search for
me with all your heart, you will find me!"*

JEREMIAH 29:13

Some days, it feels hard to find God. Don't worry—He's still with you, but He's teaching you to search for Him.

How? First, He teaches you to trust Him. Romans 8:24 says, "If we see what we are waiting for, then that is not really hope." If you could hear God speak from a burning bush the way Moses did, you wouldn't have to trust that He's really there—you'd hear Him with your own ears. So sometimes God stays silent so you'll search for Him.

Second, God teaches you to depend on Him, not yourself or anyone else. He controls *everything* with His awesome power, and He wants you to understand that. So sometimes He'll allow a problem into your life that only He can fix to remind you to depend on Him.

So when God feels far way, search for Him with all your heart—He promises to be found!

*Lord, I will keep searching for You, because I believe
Your promise that I will find You, amen.*

TODAY WITH JESUS . . . SEARCH FOR HIM IN HIS WORD.

165

GOD SPEAKS

"I will put my teachings in their minds. And I will write them on their hearts. I will be their God, and they will be my people."
JEREMIAH 31:33

Do you ever wish God would talk right to you? That you could hear His voice and know what He wants you to do? The fact is God *does* speak to you. And the main way He does it is through His Word, the Bible.

Though the Bible was written by men, it was inspired by God's Holy Spirit. That means God told them what to write. The Bible tells you who God is, how He works for and through His people, how much He loves you, and how He wants you to live. In the Bible you'll find everything God wants to tell you—and everything you need to know.

Whether you're facing a problem, your heart is broken, or you're having a wonderful day, open the Bible and let God speak to you. His words will be exactly what you need to hear.

Dear God, help me hear what You want to tell me through Your Word, amen.

TODAY WITH JESUS . . . LISTEN FOR GOD'S VOICE AS YOU READ HIS WORD.

SAY THAT AGAIN

*"Whom can I send? Who will go for us?" So
I said, "Here I am. Send me!"*

ISAIAH 6:8

Do you ever find the same Bible verses popping up over and over again? Maybe you heard them first in a sermon, then your dad talked about them, and you read them again in a devotional. Sometimes God leads you to the same verses over and over again. Why? Because He's trying to tell you something.

God uses His Word to speak to you. Perhaps you've prayed about a decision, and He's showing you the way to go. Or perhaps He's pointing out a sin you need to confess. God might have a special job for you, or maybe He's reminding you of how much He loves and treasures you. Through the verses of the Bible, God will guide, challenge, warn, and comfort you.

So when you see the same verses popping up over and over again, pay close attention . . . because God is speaking to you.

*Father, thank You for Your Word. Please help me
hear when You're speaking to me, amen.*

**TODAY WITH JESUS . . . PAY CLOSE ATTENTION
WHEN GOD REPEATS HIMSELF.**

SACRIFICE AND BLESSING

"The foxes have holes to live in. The birds have nests to live in. But the Son of Man has no place where he can rest his head."
MATTHEW 8:20

God will never ask you to sacrifice—or to give up—anything without giving you an even greater blessing in return. After all, that's what He did for His very own Son, Jesus.

Think about it: Jesus gave up all the riches of His home in heaven to come and live a poor man's life and then die on the cross. Jesus did that to save you, but He also received a blessing in return. What was it? *The blessing of you.* That's right—for Jesus, the blessing of having you with Him for all eternity was worth all His sacrifices. That's how great His love for you is.

So when God asks you to give up something that's important to you—your time, your money, your comfort—remember that He understands how hard it is. But trust Him to bless you with something even better.

Dear God, I know that Jesus gave up everything for me. Help me be willing to give up anything for You, amen.

TODAY WITH JESUS . . . TRUST HIM WITH WHAT'S MOST IMPORTANT TO YOU.

KNOWING JESUS

I want to know Christ and experience the mighty
power that raised him from the dead.
PHILIPPIANS 3:10 NLT

Jesus wants you to know who He is and to understand how holy, majestic, and powerful He is. He wants you to know His love, grace, and joy. Why? Because when you know who Jesus is, then you're better able to live for Him and serve Him. He makes life worthwhile.

The apostle Paul said his greatest goal was to "know Christ." And Paul did know Him. So even when Paul was lied about, rejected, stoned, beaten, arrested, and shipwrecked, he could say, "The Lord stayed with me. He gave me strength. . . . The Lord will bring me safely to his heavenly kingdom" (2 Timothy 4:17–18). Knowing Jesus gave Paul courage, strength, and joy.

And when you know who Jesus is, He'll give you His courage, strength, and joy, too, no matter what you face. Jesus is more than your Savior. He's also your comforter, forgiver, healer, Prince of Peace, and greatest friend.

Jesus, I want to know You. Show me who You really are, amen.

TODAY WITH JESUS . . . OPEN UP HIS
WORD AND GET TO KNOW HIM.

WHO YOU REALLY ARE

*Christ made us right with God; he made us pure
and holy, and he freed us from sin.*
1 CORINTHIANS 1:30 NLT

Do you find yourself battling the same sin again and again? Maybe it's your temper or the words you use. Perhaps it's respecting your parents or being kind to your brother or sister. Part of the reason you struggle may be that you don't really understand everything Jesus did for you.

Here's the deal: because Jesus died on the cross, your sins are forgiven. But that's not all. Because of Jesus, you are *changed*. When you decide to follow Him, you are transformed from a sinner to a saint—from a person separated from God, to one blessed with His love, help, and acceptance. But if you keep thinking of yourself as a sinner, then, chances are, you'll continue making wrong choices.

See yourself as God sees you—a forgiven saint. Sometimes you may forget to ask God for help. That's okay and He will forgive you. But when you realize who you really are, you'll find it easier to live as His beloved child who has been set free from your sins.

*Lord, thank You for changing me from a sinner
to a saint. Help me not to sin, amen.*

**TODAY WITH JESUS . . . REMEMBER WHO
YOU ARE BECAUSE OF JESUS.**

ARE YOU REALLY LISTENING?

*The people of Berea . . . searched the Scriptures day after
day to see if Paul and Silas were teaching the truth.*

ACTS 17:11 NLT

When you hear someone teach about the Bible, there are two ways to listen: *just listening* and *really hearing*. If you're *just listening*, you take whatever the preacher or teacher says and accept it as the truth. But if you're *really hearing* what they say, you'll check it out for yourself. You'll take notes. You'll look up the Bible verses and ask yourself questions like:

- Do these verses really say what the preacher says they do?
- Does the lesson match God's Word?
- What is God trying to tell me through this lesson?
- How can I use what I'm learning today in my life?

When you're really listening, it's a bit like being a detective because you're also questioning, searching, and comparing what's said to what God's Word says. And when you do, God blesses your listening heart (Matthew 7:7–8).

*Dear God, I don't want to just listen—help me
really hear what You want to teach me, amen.*

**TODAY WITH JESUS . . . BE A DETECTIVE
AND SEARCH FOR GOD'S TRUTH.**

REAL PEACE

Gideon built an altar there to worship the Lord.
Gideon named the altar The Lord Is Peace.
JUDGES 6:24

If you're trying to fit in with the world, you'll never have peace. To get real peace—to be free from worry, fear, and stress—you must please God, not the world.

Gideon was a Bible hero from long ago. When he lived, "everyone did what he [or she] thought was right" (Judges 21:25). This means everyone acted just the way they wanted to, and this didn't bring peace. In fact, it brought war. Israel's people were constantly being attacked.

Gideon was from the smallest, weakest tribe in Israel. So when God told him to stand up to Israel's enemies, Gideon didn't believe he could do it. And wouldn't it be easier to just try to get along with their enemies anyway? But God said, "I will be with you" (Judges 6:16). And when Gideon obeyed, God led him to victory—and to peace. He'll do the same for you. So even if it's hard and even if it's not popular, obey God, and He'll give you peace.

Lord, please bless me with Your peace as I try
to follow You and not the world, amen.

JUST DO IT

The priests who were carrying the Ark of the LORD's Covenant stood on
dry ground in the middle of the riverbed as the people passed by.
JOSHUA 3:17 NLT

The Israelites had been slaves in Egypt. But even after God set them free, the Israelites disobeyed Him by refusing to go into the land He had promised them. Then, after forty years of wandering in the desert, they at last turned their hearts to God and He led them toward the promised land again. This time, they were ready to obey God.

So when God told them to take the ark of the covenant—their most beloved symbol of His presence—into the middle of the Jordan River, they did it, even though they were scared. And because they obeyed, God parted the waters and the people walked across on dry ground.

When you obey God, He blesses you. So no matter what He tells you to do—whether it's to love your enemy, say you're sorry, forgive, or be kind—just do it. You may be afraid. What He says may not make sense. But do it anyway. And then watch for all the ways He blesses you.

God, I want to do what You say. Help me
obey You—no matter what, amen.

TODAY WITH JESUS . . . DO WHAT GOD SAYS.

WHEN YOU CAN'T SLEEP

That same night the king could not sleep. So he gave an order
for the daily court record to be brought in and read to him.
ESTHER 6:1

Do you ever feel restless or have trouble falling asleep? You just can't stop thinking about what happened that day—or worrying about what might happen tomorrow. One reason this might happen is because God has something to tell you.

In the book of Esther, King Xerxes was tricked into signing a law that would destroy the Jewish people. And so, a few nights later, when the king couldn't sleep, he called for the record of his court's history to be read to him. As it was read, he found a mistake in it. Reading that mistake—and fixing it—helped save the Jewish people.

If you can't sleep and you can't figure out why, ask yourself if God is trying to tell you something. Sometimes God uses your restlessness to get your attention. The best thing to do is stop and pray. Ask God what He's trying to say.

Lord, when I'm feeling restless and I can't sleep,
show me what I need to do, amen.

TODAY WITH JESUS . . . IF YOU'RE
FEELING RESTLESS, TALK TO GOD.

LISTEN

*The warning of a wise person is valuable to someone
who will listen. It is worth as much as gold.*
PROVERBS 25:12

Naaman had a terrible skin disease, so he went to God's prophet Elisha, hoping to be healed. Elisha sent a messenger to tell Naaman to wash in the Jordan River seven times. But Naaman was proud and the Jordan River was dirty, so he refused. *Until* . . . his servants said, "If the prophet had told you to do some great thing, wouldn't you have done it?" (2 Kings 5:13). So why not do this simple thing? Naaman listened to his servants. He obeyed and was healed.

Sometimes, God will use another person to tell you what you need to hear. Of course, you must make sure that person's words match God's Word. For example, God won't have someone tell you to get revenge when His Word says to forgive. But if a person's words match God's Word, then pay attention. Never be too proud to listen or to obey—so that you won't miss out on God's great blessings.

*Lord, please help me know when You are speaking
to me through someone else, amen.*

TODAY WITH JESUS . . . LISTEN FOR GOD'S MESSAGES.

A LOT TO LEARN

My dear children, I write this letter to you so that you will not sin. But if anyone does sin, we have Jesus Christ. . . . He defends us before God the Father.
1 JOHN 2:1

You're young, and you know you still have a lot to learn to be a grown-up—things like how to drive, how to pay bills, and how to work at a job. In the same way, when you decide to follow God, you become a child of God. And as a *child* of God, He knows that you have a lot to learn—things like how to pray and study His Word, how to listen to Him, and how to obey Him.

God also knows that because you're a child, you're still learning, and sometimes you're going to get it wrong. Don't worry. God doesn't expect you to be perfect. He won't love you less because you mess up. In fact, He sent His Son, Jesus, to help you, to save you, and to take away your sins. That's all part of God's grace—and it's big enough to cover all your mistakes!

God, thank You for understanding that I'm still learning. And thank You for sending Jesus to forgive my sins and mistakes, amen.

TODAY WITH JESUS . . . BE THANKFUL FOR GOD'S GRACE.

ACCEPT GOD'S ANSWERS

To keep me from becoming proud, I was given a thorn in my flesh, a messenger from Satan to torment me.

2 CORINTHIANS 12:7 NLT

God always answers your prayers. And His answers are always perfect. But . . . His answers aren't always the ones *you* want, and they don't always come when *you* want them.

Just ask the apostle Paul. He had a problem. He called it a "thorn" (2 Corinthians 12:7), and he asked God to take it away. But God didn't take it away. Paul kept asking and asking until, at last, he understood that God was using that "thorn" to teach him to depend on Him.

Sometimes, God will answer your prayer by saying *no* or *not right now*. When He does, talk to Him about it. Ask God if you're praying for the wrong thing, or if you haven't obeyed Him in some way. Then accept His answer. And remember: when God says *no* or *not now*, it's because He has something much better waiting for you and He doesn't want you to miss it.

*Lord, help me accept Your answers and trust
that You want only the best for me, amen.*

**TODAY WITH JESUS . . . TRUST THAT
GOD'S ANSWERS ARE BEST.**

INVITE GOD

Happy is the person who . . . loves the Lord's teachings.
He thinks about those teachings day and night.
PSALM 1:1–2

Every day, you have a choice to make: invite God to be part of your life by spending time with Him in prayer and in His Word, *or* leave Him out and live your life on your own. With God, you'll find peace and strength. But on your own, you'll find worry, fear, and stress.

When you decide to follow God, He doesn't promise everything will be easy. But He does promise to bless you—by always loving you and being there for you. He gives you His wisdom, so that you know things like how to be a good friend, how to honor your parents, how to be a good sport, and how to help others. God changes the way you think about things, and He fills you with His goodness, strength, and peace so you can face any trouble.

So invite God into your life today—by talking to Him and reading His Word.

Dear God, I want You to be in every part of my life.
Use Your Word to show me how to live, amen.

TODAY WITH JESUS . . . TALK TO GOD
ABOUT EVERY PART OF YOUR LIFE.

GOD USES THE UNUSUAL

Moses saw that the bush was on fire, but it was not burning up.

EXODUS 3:2

Moses had seen lots of fires and lots of bushes on fire. But he'd never seen a bush that burned . . . and didn't burn up! When he stopped to investigate, God spoke to him. God had wanted to get Moses' attention, so He did it by using the unusual.

God uses unusual things to get our eyes and our hearts to focus on Him. When you're a child of God, there's no such thing as an accident or a coincidence. An unexpected change at school, a friend's surprise gift, even an emergency—nothing surprises God. In fact, God just might be using that unusual thing to get your attention.

The next time you're surprised—whether it's a good surprise or a not-so-good shock—talk to God about it. Ask Him if there's something He'd like to tell you. Learn to look for Him in *every* situation you face—especially the unusual ones.

Lord, help me see every situation in my life
as a chance to talk to You, amen.

**TODAY WITH JESUS . . . LOOK FOR GOD
IN EVERY PART OF YOUR DAY.**

WHEN YOU FAIL

*Joshua tore his clothes in sorrow. He bowed facedown on the
ground before the Ark of the LORD and stayed there until evening.*
JOSHUA 7:6 NCV

The Israelites had just defeated the great city of Jericho with its
towering wall. Now, they were ready to attack Ai, a tiny town that
should be easy to capture. But there was a problem: the Israelites
hadn't obeyed God. So God let His people be defeated. It was a terrible
loss, but it reminded the people that their strength came from obeying God. And it made Joshua turn to God for help.

There's a huge difference between failing and being a failure.
You're only a *failure* if you stop trying. But *failing* can actually lead to
success—if it makes you turn to God for help.

When you fail at something you're trying to do, talk to God about
it. Thank Him for using it to get your attention, and ask Him to help
you. Then let that time of failing be the beginning of a future victory
with God.

*Father, it's hard to be thankful for the times I fail, but I
trust You to use them to help me succeed, amen.*

TODAY WITH JESUS . . . LEARN FROM YOUR MISTAKES.

WHAT YOU NEED MOST

Israel became very poor because of the Midianites.
So the Israelites cried out to the Lord for help.

JUDGES 6:6

The stories in the book of Judges all start with the same problem: "Everyone did what he thought was right" (17:6)—instead of what God said was right. This caused all sorts of sin. Because of that sin, God would allow hard times to fall upon the people until they finally turned back to Him for help.

What made the Israelites turn back to God? When God took away the things of this world—their money, their stuff, even their food—that's what got their attention. Has God taken something away from you? Money or things? Friends, sports, or popularity? If so, He might be trying to get your attention. Have the things of this world become more important to you than God?

God promises to "give you everything you need" (Philippians 4:19), and He will. But He also knows your greatest need is for Him. Put Him first—not the things of this world.

God, You're more important than anything in this
world. Help my life to show that, amen.

TODAY WITH JESUS . . . PUT GOD FIRST.

WHEN YOU'RE SICK

At that time Hezekiah became very sick. . . . He
prayed to the Lord. And the Lord spoke to him.
2 CHRONICLES 32:24

I t's hard to be sick. You feel tired and terrible. And you might even wonder if you'll ever get better. But God is so powerful that He can bring a blessing even out of the times you feel sick.

How? Being sick forces you to be still, and that gives you time to think. So think about God. Talk to Him. Yes, ask Him to heal you, but also ask Him about other things, like what He wants you to know about Him and how He wants you to serve Him. Read His Word—or listen to a recording of it, if you don't feel like reading. Let God use even your times of sickness to bring you closer to Him. And if it's someone else who's sick, show them God's love by helping and serving.

God has wonderful plans for all the times of your life—even the times of sickness.

Lord, thank You for using all the times of my life—even
times of sickness—to pull me closer to You, amen.

TODAY WITH JESUS . . . PAY ATTENTION TO GOD.

IS THAT GOD TALKING?

"My sheep listen to my voice. I know them, and they follow me."
JOHN 10:27

There are lots of voices talking around you. Parents, teachers, friends, and just random kids in the hallway. God is also one of those voices, but how do you know when He's speaking?

First, understand that God really is speaking to you. And He wants you to hear Him, but you need to learn to *recognize* His voice. How? By spending time with Him. Just as you know your best friend's voice because of all the great conversations you've had together, you'll recognize God's voice when you spend time with Him.

The next step is to read God's Word. Get to know the way He speaks and the kinds of things He says. Remember, God will never say anything that disagrees with Scripture. As you spend time with God and His Word, you'll learn His voice and you'll be able to say, "Hey, that's God talking!"

Father, teach me to hear and know Your voice
as we spend time together, amen.

TODAY WITH JESUS . . . STOP AND LISTEN TO GOD.

"GOOD GROUND"

*"But what is the seed that fell on the good ground? That seed is
like the person who hears the teaching and understands it."*
MATTHEW 13:23

What is "good ground"? For the farmer, it's soil that's been plowed up and is ready for seeds to be planted. It's rich dirt, without any weeds, that will encourage the seeds to grow strong roots and produce good crops. For children of God, "good ground" is a mind that wants to learn more about Him, and it's a heart that allows His Word to take root by loving and obeying Him.

How can you make your mind and heart "good ground" for God? Start by thinking thoughts that are "true, and honorable, and right, and pure, and lovely, and admirable" (Philippians 4:8 NLT). Don't fill your mind with the "weeds" of this world; instead, fill it with the richness of God and His Word. And then ask Jesus to help you obey Him and love Him more each day.

When your life is "good ground" for God, He'll bless you by making you grow in beautiful and amazing ways.

*Father, make my heart and my mind
"good ground" for You, amen.*

**TODAY WITH JESUS . . . THINK ABOUT
THE GOOD THINGS OF GOD.**

GOD'S NOT AFRAID OF ANYTHING

I asked the Lord for help, and he answered me.
He saved me from all that I feared.

PSALM 34:4

Fear is a terrible and powerful thing. When it grabs hold of you, it can be hard to think. Whether it's a bad dream or a tough situation, it's so very important that you take your fears straight to God.

First, ask God to show you what's *really* making you afraid. For example, if you're scared of the dark, it could be that you're really afraid of being left all alone. If you are afraid of making your friends mad, it could be that you're really scared of being rejected. Then, trust God to help you face that fear. Ask Him to use His words from the Bible to chase it away. In fact, your fears of being alone or rejected are completely defeated by His promise: "I will never leave you" (Hebrews 13:5). With God, you always have someone who loves you, accepts you, and helps you.

Whatever your fear, face it with God. He's not afraid of anything, because His power is greater than anything. Trust Him to help, protect, and take care of you.

Lord, help me understand the real reason for
my fear, and then help me face it, amen.

TODAY WITH JESUS . . . TAKE YOUR FEARS TO GOD.

BE SATISFIED

*I have learned to be satisfied with the things I
have and with everything that happens.*
PHILIPPIANS 4:11

If anybody ever had a reason to complain about his life, it was the apostle Paul. He was beaten, shipwrecked, thrown in jail more than once, and lived in constant danger. He went without sleep, food, and water too many times to count. And—just like you—he struggled to do what he knew God wanted him to do.

So how could Paul say he was "satisfied . . . with everything that happens"? How could he have peace, contentment, and even joy with a life like that? He did it by trusting God completely, and by letting God's Holy Spirit give him strength and comfort.

You can learn to be satisfied regardless of what happens, too—by trusting God completely. Then God will give you His strength and comfort. He'll help you to be content and satisfied, no matter what you have or what's happening in your life.

*Jesus, I want to be satisfied with my life.
Help me trust You completely, amen.*

TODAY WITH JESUS . . . TRUST HIM COMPLETELY.

GIVE IT TO GOD

Give all your worries to him, because he cares for you.

1 PETER 5:7

Problems happen. It's just a fact. Sometimes they're small—a pop quiz, a lost shoe, a misunderstanding. Sometimes they're big—an illness, a loss, a friend who turns against you. Problems can frustrate you and steal your joy. It's no wonder you worry about them.

But God didn't create you to worry or to handle problems all on your own. That's why He tells you to give your troubles to Him. How? Start by talking to Him. Prayer takes your attention off the problem and puts it on God, the One who can handle it. If you've done anything wrong that's added to your struggles, confess that to God. Then say to Him, "I need Your help and comfort. Be with me, take care of me, and show me what I need to do." Then trust God to handle it—He really will take care of you.

Father, I give my worries and problems to You.
Please comfort me and take care of me, amen.

TODAY WITH JESUS . . . TALK TO GOD ABOUT YOUR PROBLEMS—NO MATTER HOW BIG OR SMALL.

SPOTTING THE PHONY

"His sheep follow him because they know his voice."
JOHN 10:4 NIV

Do you know how detectives are trained to recognize counterfeit, or phony, money? They study the real thing *a lot*. Then, when they hold up the phony money against the real money, the counterfeit bills are easy to spot.

That's also the best way to recognize God's voice. Study the real thing by reading God's own words in the Bible. Then it'll be easy to spot the counterfeits because their message won't match God's words.

God will never say anything that goes against the Bible. So if that little voice—the one on television, in the halls at school, or whispering in your thoughts—says something like, "Forget what your mom says. Everybody's doing it," or, "You don't have to forgive her. She deserves what she gets," then you'll know that voice isn't from God. Don't listen! Study God's Word, so you'll be able to spot those phony voices.

Father God, please teach me to hear Your voice and to know when You're not the one who's speaking, amen.

**TODAY WITH JESUS . . . STUDY THE
REAL THING—GOD'S WORD.**

YOU'RE RICH!

*I pray that you will know that the blessings God has
promised his holy people are rich and glorious.*

EPHESIANS 1:18

Do you know what the word *heir* means? It's a person who inherits (or gets) something when someone dies. The word probably makes you think about inheriting money, gold, or jewels. But as a child of God, you're an heir to something much greater—you're an heir to heaven and the riches of God (Romans 8:16–17). And the great news is you don't have to wait for heaven to start enjoying some of those blessings!

For example, do you need strength? God has all the power you'll ever need—just ask Him to help you. Need wisdom? No one's wiser than God, and He promises to bless you with that wisdom (James 1:5). Are you worried or upset? Then He'll fill you with His joy and peace.

The riches of this world can be lost or stolen, but the blessings of God can never be taken away. When you're an heir of God, you're truly rich!

*Jesus, I'm so thankful You came and died on the
cross so that I could be an heir of heaven, amen.*

**TODAY WITH JESUS . . . THANK GOD
FOR HIS RICHES IN YOUR LIFE.**

JULY

JULY 1

GOD'S WONDERFUL THINGS

We have received God's Spirit (not the world's spirit), so we
can know the wonderful things God has freely given us.
1 CORINTHIANS 2:12 NLT

When you decide to follow Jesus, the Holy Spirit of God comes *to live inside you.* He will teach you, guide you, and help you get to know who God really is.

The Bible says the Holy Spirit will also help you "know the wonderful things God has freely given us." That means the Spirit will fill you with all the blessings of God—like love, joy, and peace. And other things, like the strength to get through hard times, the wisdom to know what's right, and the courage to do it. And the very best thing the Spirit will give you is the ability to know Jesus Himself—who He is and how much He loves you.

How does the Spirit do all this? Through God's Word. When you spend time reading the Bible, praying, and quietly listening for His soft whispers, that's when He fills you up with God's "wonderful things."

> *Dear God, thank You for the wonderful gift of Your*
> *Holy Spirit. Help me to let Him lead me, amen.*

TODAY WITH JESUS . . . THINK ABOUT THE
WONDERFUL THINGS HE HAS GIVEN YOU.

THE BATTLE WITH SIN

God . . . will not allow the temptation to be more than you can stand. When you are tempted, he will show you a way out.

1 CORINTHIANS 10:13 NLT

Y ou are in a battle with sin. Every day, there are temptations all around you. But God gives you everything you need to win the battle against sin—every time! But you must do your part:

1. Admit when you're tempted to do wrong. Then, remember God is stronger than that temptation.
2. Think about what would happen if you gave in to that sin. For example, if you cheated on a test, what kind of problems would that cause?
3. Sin tries to tempt you with worry and fear. For example, are you tempted to cheat because you're worried about getting a bad grade? Don't let fear push you into sin. Do what's right and remember God's promise to take care of you.

Turn to God when sin is tempting. Ask Him to help you—He always will.

Lord, You know I struggle with temptations, but I also know You'll help me defeat them, amen.

TODAY WITH JESUS . . . TURN TO GOD WHEN YOU'RE TEMPTED TO DO WRONG.

JULY 3

JUST ASK GOD

You do not get what you want because you do not ask God.
JAMES 4:2

Are you ever afraid to ask God for what you want? Do you think your hopes and dreams aren't important enough to take to Him? If so, then you need to know this: God loves you, and because He loves you, He's interested in *everything* about you. So go ahead and ask God for what you're dreaming of. If you don't, you just might miss out on a blessing.

Of course, God may say yes to what you want—almost as soon as you ask Him. *Or* He may ask you to wait a little while for His perfect timing. *Or* He may show you that what you want isn't good for you, and He has something much better planned for you instead.

God may not answer the way you hope or when you hope, but He will always answer. Talk to God about your hopes and dreams—He loves you and He's listening.

*Lord, thank You for always listening to me. I
know I can tell You anything, amen.*

**TODAY WITH JESUS . . . TELL GOD
YOUR HOPES AND DREAMS.**

PRAY FOR YOUR COUNTRY

Happy is the nation whose God is the Lord.

PSALM 33:12

The Fourth of July is a day of celebration—of picnics and fireworks and fun. But make sure it's also a day of prayer. Whether everything is great or not-so-great, whether this country is at war or at peace, no matter what's happening, it's important to ask God to bless and guide this nation.

What should you pray for? First, pray for all those who don't know Jesus. Ask God to help them come to know Him, because a country filled with people and leaders who love God will be a blessed place to live. And second, pray that God will protect this country from natural disasters, like hurricanes, tornadoes, and earthquakes; that He would defeat our enemies—people who would harm us, but also any evil counsel that is against His will; and that He would safeguard the soldiers who defend us.

Bow down before God, and ask Him to bless this country. Because when people turn to God, pray to Him, and obey Him, He promises to bless their land (2 Chronicles 7:14).

Lord, I pray for my country today. Protect us and help everyone to follow You, amen.

TODAY WITH JESUS . . . PRAY FOR YOUR COUNTRY.

YOU'RE IMPORTANT TO GOD

Even if my father and mother abandon me,
the Lᴏʀᴅ will hold me close.
PSALM 27:10 NLT

People can be mean sometimes—even cruel. They can say and do things that hurt your feelings and make you feel as if you don't matter. When you're left out or someone refuses to be your friend, you might even start to think things like, *I'll never be good enough*, or, *No one will ever like me*. These thoughts are lies, but they can still cause terrible hurt.

Remember this: when you are a follower of Jesus, you belong to God. He loves you no matter what, He always wants to be with you, and He will help you do wonderful things. God even sends His Holy Spirit to live inside you, so that you have a helper with you all the time.

When you're left out and lonely, what should you do? Talk to God. Let Him take away the hurts and show you how very important you are to Him.

Jesus, I'm so thankful that I'm important to
You. Thank You for loving me, amen.

TODAY WITH JESUS . . . READ LUKE 12:6–7.
WHAT DOES GOD KNOW ABOUT YOU?

A CURE FOR THE BLAHS

*Everything you say and everything you do should all
be done for Jesus your Lord. And in all you do, give
thanks to God the Father through Jesus.*

COLOSSIANS 3:17

Do you ever get "the blahs"? You have a ton of stuff to do, but you just don't care if you get it done. *What's the point?* you wonder. You're fed up and bored with it all—and maybe feeling a little bit lazy. That's a serious case of "the blahs."

But curing "the blahs" is as simple as doing the next right thing—and doing it as if it were for God. Do your homework as if God assigned it. Clean your room as if God were coming to visit. Practice as if God were watching in the stands. And then thank God for the chance to do it.

When you're doing your best and your heart is thankful, it's impossible to stay fed up or bored. So close your eyes, think about God, and thank Him for everything you can think of—and "the blahs" won't stand a chance.

*Lord, please help me to do everything today
as if I were doing it for You, amen.*

**TODAY WITH JESUS . . . THANK GOD FOR
EVERYTHING YOU GET TO DO.**

PEACE IN A PRISON

*The Lord will save me when anyone tries to hurt me. The
Lord will bring me safely to his heavenly kingdom.*
2 TIMOTHY 4:18

The apostle Paul sat locked in a prison cell because he had spoken about Jesus. He could have felt sorry for himself, but he didn't. Instead, he wrote letters and encouraged his friends to love and trust God—even to be joyful in times of trouble.

Peace is the last emotion you'd expect Paul to feel in prison, but that's exactly what he had—a peace from God "so great that we cannot understand it" (Philippians 4:7). How did Paul have peace? Because he *knew God*. Paul didn't just know *about* God; he had a personal relationship with God as his Lord, Savior, and friend. No matter what he suffered, Paul knew God's power, wisdom, and peace would be with him.

And that same power, wisdom, and peace is there for you. No matter what's happening around you, God is working through you and your life—often in ways you cannot see or understand. Trust Him because He's always there for you.

*Father, no matter what's happening, I know You
are with me. I trust You, Lord, amen.*

**TODAY WITH JESUS . . . ASK GOD TO
FILL YOU WITH HIS PEACE.**

YOU ARE WHAT YOU THINK

Think about the things of heaven, not the things of earth.
COLOSSIANS 3:2 NLT

Have you ever heard the saying, "You are what you eat"? Well, it's true for more than just food. It's also true for your thoughts. If you struggle with thoughts slipping into your mind—thoughts you know you shouldn't be thinking—then you might want to look at what you've been feeding your brain.

If you're constantly playing violent video games, then violent thoughts are more likely to pop into your mind. Or if you watch a lot of YouTube videos or movies with bad language, it's easy for bad words to slip into your thoughts—and then out your mouth!

If you want to be all God created you to be, then you need to fill your mind with things that are good and pure and holy (Philippians 4:8). Feed your mind a steady diet of God's Word. Then ask Him to sort through your thoughts and help you toss out anything that doesn't belong.

Jesus, fill my mind with thoughts about You and Your love—
and toss out any thoughts that don't belong, amen.

TODAY WITH JESUS . . . KEEP HIM IN YOUR THOUGHTS.

YOU ALWAYS HAVE HOPE

We hope in the living God. He is the Savior of all people.
1 TIMOTHY 4:10

No matter what's happening in the world or in your life, you *always* have hope that things will be better . . . because your God is alive. You can be brave because God will fight for you and will help you through every struggle. Remember, through Jesus, He has already defeated every enemy (Revelation 17:14).

That's the joy of being a Christian. Once you decide to follow Him and believe His promises (2 Corinthians 1:20), you know you can handle anything because God is with you. You have a defender who is unbeatable, you have God's never-failing love, and one day you will inherit all the blessings of heaven.

So if you're facing trouble—a small one that just won't go away or a huge one that seems to have you beat—remember that God is alive and working for your good. Trust Him to get you through.

Jesus, You are a mighty warrior and my victorious
Savior. I know You'll never let me down, amen.

**TODAY WITH JESUS . . . REMEMBER HE'S
ALIVE AND WORKING IN YOUR LIFE.**

STEPPING ON YOUR TOES

*Christ loved the church. He gave up his life for her to make her
holy and clean, washed by the cleansing of God's word.*

EPHESIANS 5:25–26 NLT

When you read the Bible, do you ever feel . . . *uncomfortable*? Or like you wish you could hide from God? That's because God uses His Word to point out things you need to work on. He might show you that you need to forgive someone or be more careful with your words. Or He might point out your bad attitude toward obeying your parents or how you need to be a more thoughtful friend.

When God "steps on your toes," you might be tempted to just skip reading His Word. Don't! The Bible is God's most powerful tool for changing you to be more like Jesus (Romans 12:2).

So open up the Bible. Ask God to teach you and show you the things you need to change. Because when your heart is willing to listen and change, God will do great things through you.

Lord, please use Your Word to make me more like Jesus, amen.

**TODAY WITH JESUS . . . FEEL
COMFORTABLE WITH YOUR BIBLE.**

BE CHANGED

God knew them before he made the world. And
God chose them to be like his Son.
ROMANS 8:29

God wants you to look more and more like Him—not in the shape of your nose or the color of your eyes, but in your love and kindness and joy. Through His words in the Bible, God shows you who He is and then asks you to make a choice: change to be more like Him, or stay the way you are.

You see, God didn't give us the Bible just for all its wonderful stories. The Bible is the way God speaks to you and tells you who He wants you to be. So today, think about this: Are you refusing to let God change you? Or are you letting the truth of His Word transform you to be more like Him? Don't let the Bible be just another book you read. Let it soak into your heart, rule your thoughts, and change you . . . to be more like Him.

Lord, open my eyes and my heart to Your Word. Let it
change me and make me who You want me to be, amen.

CHOOSE GOD

Guide me in your truth. Teach me, my God,
my Savior. I trust you all day long.

PSALM 25:5

God doesn't force you to do anything—not even what's best for you. He lets you choose whether to follow Him. That's a powerful gift *and* a huge responsibility. Every day, you'll be faced with one choice after another. Some will be small, but some will be big. Some will honor God, and some won't. Some will lead you closer to God and the life He wants for you, but others will pull you away.

One of the most powerful choices you'll ever make is trusting God and asking Him to guide you through all your decisions. And if that's the choice you want to make, then pray to be more like Him and for Him to to use every good thing, every trouble, and every moment of your life to teach you who He is and how to live in a way that pleases Him.

Lord, please guide me through every choice I
make. Help me to follow You always, amen.

TODAY WITH JESUS . . . CHOOSE HIM.

DON'T DO ALL THE TALKING

As you enter the house of God, keep your ears open.
ECCLESIASTES 5:1 NLT

D o you know someone who likes to do all the talking? It's hard to be friends with that person because you never get a chance to say what you think!

But . . . do you do that to God? When you pray, do you do all the talking? Does God get a chance to tell you what He thinks? Yes, it's important to tell God everything, but it's just as important to sit quietly and let Him tell you what's on His mind. No, you probably won't hear a big, booming voice from heaven—God doesn't usually speak that way. But He may remind you of a Bible verse you need to practice in your life, show you a sin you need to confess, or remind you of someone who needs your help. In other words, God *will* guide you (Proverbs 3:6).

But first . . . you have to listen.

Lord, I will be quiet and listen for Your voice.
Speak to me. I am listening, amen.

TODAY WITH JESUS . . . TALK TO GOD, AND THEN LISTEN.

ARE YOU READY TO CHANGE?

Do not live as you lived in the past. But be holy
in all that you do, just as God is holy.
1 PETER 1:14–15

Is there something you need to change in your life? Maybe it's the way you treat your friends—or those who aren't your friends. Maybe it's your attitude toward homework or chores. Or maybe it's the time you spend with God. Are you willing to say, "God, I want to please You. My way isn't working—I want to live Your way"?

If you're ready to make some changes, ask God to show you where to start—where you're being sinful, selfish, or just plain wrong. Whatever He brings into your mind, admit that He's right and decide to follow His ways instead. His Word will show you how with commands like "love your neighbor," "forgive others," and "be kind always." Deciding to obey God and then actually doing it will not only change your life, it will bring you wonderfully closer to Him.

Jesus, please show me what You want me
to do. I want to obey You, amen.

TODAY WITH JESUS . . . LIVE GOD'S WAY.

JUST BE HIS

I do believe! Help me to believe more!
MARK 9:24

There will be days when absolutely everything seems to go wrong. You're trying to remember God is with you and to believe He's helping you, but you just don't see it. You're tired, and you're hurt, and you're wondering if your faith is strong enough—if God really is going to come through for you this time.

But understand this: if you're wondering about God and waiting for Him to help you, then you already have enough faith to get through this. How? Because you still believe God has the answers and He'll help you (Hebrews 11:6)—even if you don't see it right now. You only need a speck—a mustard seed—of faith to overcome the troubles you're facing. God will supply the rest. Because your faith isn't about how strong you are; it's about how much you trust and depend on God.

You don't have to be strong; you just have to be His (2 Timothy 2:13). Voice your trust in Him today.

*Lord, I do trust You. Please help me to
be completely Yours, amen.*

**TODAY WITH JESUS . . . TRUST HIM TO
MAKE YOUR FAITH STRONG.**

THIS IS A TEST

These troubles come to prove that your faith is pure.
This purity of faith is worth more than gold.
1 PETER 1:7

Sometimes you'll face troubles that are bigger than you are, and you'll have absolutely no idea what to do. Everything in you will say, "Just give up!"

But don't do it. Why? Because you are right in the middle of a faith test. God isn't punishing you, and He hasn't forgotten about you. He is giving you the chance to prove you trust Him. And by trusting Him, your faith will grow even stronger.

Decide right now to trust God, no matter what happens. When things look bad, don't look at the world around you or listen to what it says about your troubles. Listen to God, because Jesus really is the answer for everything you need. There's no trouble too big, no problem too pesky, and no pit too deep that He can't rescue you. Expect Him to . . . and He will.

Lord, some troubles are just too big for me, but I'm
so thankful that nothing is too big for You! Amen.

TODAY WITH JESUS . . . REMEMBER HE'S ALWAYS THE PERFECT ANSWER.

WHAT GOD REALLY WANTS FROM YOU

"Live so that [others] will praise your Father in heaven."
MATTHEW 5:16

If you ever feel you just can't do what God wants you to do, think about this: what God expects of you is different from what you might think. What God really wants is this:

- *An open heart* that listens to Him and is ready to follow Him.
- *An eagerness to serve*—to put Him first, others second, and yourself last.
- *A selfless spirit* that gives without expecting anything in return.
- *A soul that seeks Him* and puts His goals for your life ahead of your own.
- *A willingness to do the right thing*, even when it would be easier not to.

Don't worry about what *you* can or cannot do. Trust God to show you the amazing things *He* can do through you.

Lord, thank You for choosing me to serve You, amen.

**TODAY WITH JESUS . . . TRUST HIM
TO WORK THROUGH YOU.**

LIVE IT OUT

The teaching about the cross seems foolish to those who are lost. But to us who are being saved it is the power of God.

1 CORINTHIANS 1:18

God's Word has a power no other book has . . . because it contains the living words of God Himself. They are "living words" because they actively work in your life. For example, when you're hurting, perhaps you read Psalm 23 and remember God watches over you. Or when you're lonely, you remember Jesus is always with you (Matthew 28:20).

But God's Word doesn't just work to help you—it also works to teach others about Him as you live it out. For example, when you're kind to an enemy as Matthew 5:44 teaches, you tell others about God's kindness. When you forgive as Colossians 3:13 says, you teach about how God forgives. And when you help those who can't help themselves (James 1:27), you show how much God loves and cares.

So, yes, read God's Word, but do more than that—live it out. Because that's when you really tell people about Him.

Jesus, please help me live out Your Word. Use my life to tell others about You, amen.

TODAY WITH JESUS . . . LET HOW YOU LIVE TELL OTHERS ABOUT HIM.

CAN I ASK FOR ANYTHING?

"If you ask me for anything in my name, I will do it."
JOHN 14:14

When the Bible says, "If you ask me for anything in my name, I will do it," does it really mean *anything*? If you ask for that new game or bike, for your friend not to move away, or to get a particular teacher at school next year, does that verse mean God will always say yes?

Well . . . no. Look at the middle part of the verse. You must ask *in His name*. And that means more than just saying, "in Jesus' name, amen." It means that when you pray, you're asking Jesus to shape your requests to match His character, His values, His plans, and His will. You can't do that on your own, but the Holy Spirit will help you: "the Spirit himself speaks to God for us" (Romans 8:26). As you pray in Jesus' name, letting the Spirit guide and shape your requests, the Lord will answer.

Holy Spirit, please guide my prayers. Change my heart so that I want what Jesus wants, amen.

TODAY WITH JESUS . . . ASK THE HOLY SPIRIT TO GUIDE YOUR PRAYERS.

DON'T MISS OUT

"Come to the Lord and live."

AMOS 5:6

Even though you're young, life can still be pretty stressful, even frightening. Do you ever wish someone would just take away your fears? Or give you a new way to think about the stuff that's stressing you out? Parents can often help, and friends too. But God will *always* help. He wants to listen, take away your fears, and smooth out your stressful days. But you have to let Him—by taking time to sit quietly with His Word so He can speak to you and teach you His ways.

You may think you don't have time to sit with God. You're so busy with school, family stuff, practices, and friends. But if you're always too busy, you'll not only miss out on God's help, but also His joy, peace, power, love, and wisdom. *You'll miss out on getting to know God.* Don't do it . . . make time for God.

Father, help me take time to sit quietly with You
and hear what You want to tell me, amen.

TODAY WITH JESUS . . . SIT QUIETLY
WITH HIM AND HIS WORD.

GO TO GOD

I cry out to God Most High, to the God who does everything for me.
PSALM 57:2

"I want to do it myself!" Whether it's tying your shoe or riding a bike, as you grow up you want to do things for yourself. And it's good to learn to be independent. After all, you don't want to be a grown-up who can't tie their own shoes!

But have you ever found yourself saying, "I want to do it myself" to God? Maybe not with your words, but with the way you act? You come up with a plan. You work to make it happen. Then, when things don't go as you'd planned, you worry and work some more. But do you ever stop to talk to God about it?

God *wants* you to depend on Him. He wants to be your strength, your Guide, and your all. Let Him help you and lead you in His plans . . . they're greater than anything you could plan on your own.

> *Lord, forgive me for trying to do it all by myself. I know I need You. Please guide me today, amen.*

TODAY WITH JESUS . . . LET GOD HELP YOU.

LOVE AND FORGIVE

Love each other deeply. Love has a way of not looking at others' sins.

1 PETER 4:8

When someone hurts your feelings, it's easy to just sit and think about what they did and how much it hurt you. It's easy . . . but it's not what God wants. He wants you to forgive.

Think about David. If anyone ever had a right to be angry, it was David. When he was just a young man, he saved King Saul and Israel by slaying Goliath. He faithfully served Saul by playing music to soothe the king's troubled spirit. David never did anything wrong to Saul. But Saul was so jealous of David that he tried to kill him. But did David hate Saul or try to get revenge? No. David forgave him, and God blessed him for it.

God wants you to forgive others, too—just as He forgives you. Don't hate or try to get even. Love and forgive, and God will bless you for it.

Jesus, please help me to put aside my anger and hurt and to forgive just as You forgive me, amen.

TODAY WITH JESUS . . . CHOOSE TO FORGIVE.

DON'T HIDE

I heard you walking in the garden. I was afraid
because I was naked. So I hid.
GENESIS 3:10

When you were younger, did you ever do something you knew was wrong and then try to hide from your mom or dad? Maybe it was knocking over a lamp or writing on a wall. You felt ashamed and probably a little frightened, so you hid.

Adam did the same thing when he ate the forbidden fruit—he tried to hide from God. But when God asked, "Where are you?" (Genesis 3:9), it wasn't because He didn't know where Adam was. Of course He knew! God wanted Adam to admit *why* he was hiding.

When you do wrong, don't hide or make excuses. Go to God so He can forgive you and take away your shame and fear. God knows the past, present, and future, so He already knows every sin you'll ever commit. And He still loves you! Don't hide—run to Him and let Him heal you.

> *Father, I've been hiding _____ from You because*
> *I was ashamed. Please forgive me, amen.*

**TODAY WITH JESUS . . . WHEN YOU
MESS UP, RUN TO HIM.**

A PRICE TO PAY

The Lord God forced the man out of the garden of Eden.
He had to work the ground he was taken from.

GENESIS 3:23

When Adam and Eve sinned by eating the forbidden fruit, there was a price to pay. They had to leave their home in the garden of Eden. They had to work hard for their food. Sickness, sin, and death became part of their lives. All these troubles happened because they didn't obey God.

In the same way, when you do wrong, there is a price to pay. If you cheat on a test, you'll flunk. If you treat a friend badly, you'll lose that friend. If you are rude to your parents, you'll be grounded. When you don't obey God, He'll still love you, and, if you ask, He'll forgive you. But there will still be consequences. Those consequences aren't just to punish you—they're to teach you not to choose the wrong way again.

That's why it's so important to listen to God and obey Him. It'll make your life *so* much better and blessed.

Lord, if I'm headed in the wrong direction, please
show me. I want to obey You, amen.

TODAY WITH JESUS . . . OBEY HIM.

GOD FIRST

All things are worth nothing compared with the greatness of knowing Christ Jesus my Lord.
PHILIPPIANS 3:8

What kinds of thoughts are filling up your mind today? What kinds of things are filling up your time? Your answers to those questions say a lot about what's really important to you.

For example, are your thoughts full of worries and fears—or God? Do you spend time thinking about your favorite TV show, the big game, or hanging out with friends, but not God? Does your day have time for school, sports, TV, friends, YouTube, video games, and pretty much everything *except* God? Be warned: when you fill your mind and day with everything *but* God, then frustration and trouble are sure to follow. Putting other things before God steals your peace, your energy, and your joy.

Put God first. Spend time with Him and His Word. Include Him in everything. When you do, He'll bless you, and everything else in your life will be so much better.

Lord, show me the things that I'm putting before You and help me put You first instead, amen.

TODAY WITH JESUS . . . PUT HIM FIRST.

WHAT DOES GOD WANT?

We ask God that you will know fully what God wants. We pray that you
will also have great wisdom and understanding in spiritual things.

COLOSSIANS 1:9

When you're trying to figure out which choice to make, do you ask yourself, *What does God want?* Because it's the most important question of all.

You can ask what choice would be best or easiest or make your parents happy. But you won't make the best decision until you've asked God what He wants. And it's not as hard to figure out as you might think. God wants you to obey Him—and He's eager to help you do just that.

First, talk to Him, read His Word, and listen to what *He says*— not the world—because God will never steer you wrong. He'll give you wisdom for every step of the way. Second, ask the Holy Spirit to change you so that you want the same things God wants. And finally, trust that the God who's mighty enough to save you, also loves you enough to teach you the way to go.

Lord, teach me what You want—and then,
please, help me to do it, amen.

TODAY WITH JESUS . . . ASK, "WHAT DOES GOD WANT?"

YOU MATTER TO HIM

God let even his own Son suffer for us. God gave his Son for us all. So with Jesus, God will surely give us all things.
ROMANS 8:32

You can count on God. No matter how big or how small your problem is, He'll never—*absolutely never*—let you down. God proved His love for you by giving up His only Son to take away your biggest problem—the sin that separates you from Him (Isaiah 59:2).

God knows you need Him, so He gave up His only Son, Jesus—who was "more important than anything in this world or in the next world" (Ephesians 1:21)—to make it possible for you to know Him. If God would give up His own Son so that you could have a relationship with Him, why would you ever doubt that He wants to help you with whatever you face? Your problems matter to God because *you* matter to Him.

The fact is, the God of all creation, the Great I AM, the King of kings and Lord of lords *loves* you. Count on Him today.

Dear God, when I think of all You gave up for me, I am so grateful. Thank You for loving me so very much, amen.

TODAY WITH JESUS . . . COUNT ON HIM.

GOD WILL

"I am God All-Powerful. Obey me and do what is right. I will make an agreement between us. I will make you the ancestor of many people."

GENESIS 17:1–2

God made a covenant, or an agreement, with Abraham. And the most important words in that covenant were "I will." If Abraham would obey Him, God would give him a son. God took responsibility for keeping His promise.

Have you asked God for something, but His answer is taking much longer than you expected? Does it seem you might never get what you asked Him for? It's tempting to take matters into your own hands. Don't! Abraham's wife, Sarah, did that, and the results were so disastrous that they're still causing wars today.

When you're tempted to fix things your own way, remember that it's God "who does everything" for you (Psalm 57:2). Your only job—just like Abraham—is to obey Him and trust Him to handle everything else. It's His responsibility to take care of all that concerns you—and He will.

Lord, help me obey You and trust You
to keep Your promises, amen.

**TODAY WITH JESUS . . . TRUST HIM
TO KEEP HIS PROMISES.**

WHEN YOU'RE THIRSTY

My soul thirsts for God, for the living God.
PSALM 42:2 NIV

Imagine you're in a desert. The sun is hot and blazing down on you. Your throat is dry, and your lips are cracked. There's not a drop of water anywhere in sight. So what's the one thing you can't stop thinking about? *Water.* It's all you want.

Your soul can also go through a desert. Troubles blaze down on you. Your heart is hurt, and your spirit is tired. God doesn't seem to be anywhere in sight. So what's the one thing you can't stop thinking about? *God.* Like a desert traveler searching for water, you look for Him everywhere, listen for Him, and thirst for His presence.

Sometimes God allows you to walk through deserts of troubles, so you'll thirst for Him and search for Him. But He promises that when you search for Him, He will be found (Jeremiah 29:13). And your thirst for Him will be satisfied (Matthew 5:6).

*Lord, I am thirsty for You. Please fill me up
with Your wonderful presence, amen.*

TODAY WITH JESUS . . . SEARCH FOR GOD.

JULY 30

FIXING YOUR FAITH

As the Scripture says, "The person who is made
right with God by faith will live forever."

ROMANS 1:17

The biggest thing that keeps your faith from growing isn't what's happening around you, it isn't your past mistakes, and it isn't anything someone else has done. It's that you don't really trust God—you don't completely believe in His wisdom and His love. And it's keeping His power from flowing into your life.

So how do you fix your faith? First, ask God to help your heart and mind be so focused on Him that whenever a problem pops us—no matter how big or small—you immediately pray for His help. Second, stop trying to be in charge. Remember that God is in control, and if He asks you to do something, then He'll give you everything you need to do it.

If you want to fix your faith and make it grow, then let go and trust God—and watch Him bless you.

Father, keep my thoughts and my heart focused on
You, especially when troubles come along, amen.

TODAY WITH JESUS . . . THINK ABOUT HIM.

WHAT GOD DOES FOR YOU

Let us look only to Jesus. He is the one
who . . . makes our faith perfect.
HEBREWS 12:2

When you're feeling surrounded by troubles and hard times, you might be tempted to doubt God. If that happens, it's time to remember who He is and all He does for you.

He is your Savior and Lord, your life-giver, protector, provider, guide, and Savior. He knows everything about you—even things you don't know about yourself! Because God is all-knowing, He always knows exactly what's best for you. And because He loves you, you can count on Him to bless you with what is best for you.

When you decide to follow God, He forgives your sins (Colossians 1:13–14), He makes your life full and complete (Colossians 2:10), and He gives you everything you need to be His faithful follower. He is Lord above all lords and King above all kings—and He loves you perfectly. Even when everything around you seems dark, trust Him to lead you to His light.

Dear God, I believe You know what's best for me,
and I trust You to bless me with it, amen.

**TODAY WITH JESUS . . . THINK ABOUT
ALL GOD DOES FOR YOU.**

AUGUST

JESUS HELPS

"My grace is all you need. My power works best in weakness."
2 CORINTHIANS 12:9 NLT

Have you ever tried to lift a big, heavy box—and just couldn't do it? No matter how hard you tried, that box wasn't going anywhere. But then a friend came along and offered to help. Suddenly that box wasn't quite so heavy anymore.

That's what Jesus does for you when you decide to follow Him. There are lots of big, heavy things in life—like worry, fear, trouble, and stress—that are impossible to carry all by yourself. But as you learn to trust and depend on Jesus, He doesn't just help you carry those things—He carries them for you. You don't have to wear yourself out trying to do things all alone.

Nobody is *always* the best. And nobody gets it right every time. In fact, it's when you need help that you have the greatest chance to grow—by learning you really can count on Jesus.

Heavenly Father, help me learn to depend on
You. I know I can always trust You, amen.

TODAY WITH JESUS . . . LET HIM CARRY YOUR LOAD.

DON'T RUSH

"Those who hear God's teaching with a good, honest heart.
They obey God's teaching and patiently produce good fruit."

LUKE 8:15

You'll find lots of wonderful advice in the Bible about making decisions. Things like: talk to God (Jeremiah 33:3), trust Him (Proverbs 3:5–6), and ask for wisdom (James 1:5). But nowhere does the Bible say you should rush into a decision. Sure, there will be times when you need to make a choice quickly, but God will never tell you to rush into something without talking to Him first.

Satan, on the other hand, wants you to be in a hurry. Why? Because if you rush through without talking to God, then you're more likely to make a bad choice—which is exactly what he wants.

When you're rushed to make a decision, force yourself to stop and talk to God. Be willing to wait for His answer. Just remember, God probably won't tell you every little detail. Instead, He'll guide you—one step at a time—to exactly where you need to be.

Dear God, guide me in my choices today. I know
You'll always lead me the right way, amen.

TODAY WITH JESUS . . . TALK TO
HIM ABOUT YOUR CHOICES.

RIGHT WITH GOD

Create in me a pure heart, God. Make my spirit right again.
PSALM 51:10

Sometimes, God points out things in your life that you need to work on. And sometimes, He does this by giving you a problem to overcome. If you struggle with anger, He may bring a difficult person into your life to teach you self-control. If you struggle with greed or selfishness, He may take away some of your "stuff" to teach you there are more important things in life than your possessions.

You may start to wonder if God is angry with you or if He still loves you. But God *never* stops loving you. In fact, He takes the time to teach you *because* He loves you. He wants to help you get rid of the sin in your life, so that you'll be clean and pure and right with Him. So when God points out a sin in your life, it's best to confess it, turn away from it, and then try to do the right thing.

Lord, please forgive me for my sins. Make me clean and pure and right with You, amen.

TODAY WITH JESUS . . . DO THE RIGHT THING.

YOU ARE LOVED

The Father has loved us so much! He loved us so much that we are called children of God.

1 JOHN 3:1

God loves you more than anyone else ever will. And He created you to love Him back and to live with Him as His child forever.

God not only loves you, but He also wants you to *understand* how much He loves you. He knows you inside and out—everything you've ever done or thought or said, and everything you'll ever do or think or say. Nothing surprises God, and nothing can make Him stop loving you. Of course, God doesn't like it when you sin, and He may allow troubles into your life to teach you. But when you confess your sins to Him, when you *repent* and turn away from those sins, God always welcomes you back with open arms (1 John 1:9).

God will *never* withhold His love from you. When you decide to follow Him, you become His very own child—a beloved child of God forever. And no one will ever be able to take you away from Him.

Lord, thank You for Your love that never ends.
Help me to follow You always, amen.

AUGUST 5

ROOTS

"Since they don't have deep roots, they don't last long."
MATTHEW 13:21 NLT

Roots make a plant strong. They sink deep down in the soil, seeking out the water and nutrients the plant needs to grow. When storms come, those deep roots keep the plant anchored safely in the ground.

In many ways, the Word of God is like the roots of your faith, and your heart is the soil. As you read from the Bible every day, the roots of your faith grow stronger. When your heart is soft and you want to learn about God, then His Word is able sink deep down inside you. It will fill you with the living water of Jesus and the nutrients of His love, joy, and peace—everything you need to grow in your faith. And when the storms of life come, you'll be safely anchored in Him—because the roots of your faith run deep.

Father, please soften up the ground of my heart,
and plant Your Word deep inside, amen.

TODAY WITH JESUS . . . PLANT GOD'S
WORD IN YOUR HEART TODAY.

PRAY BIG

*"I pray that they will all be one, just as you and I are
one—as you are in me, Father, and I am in you."*

JOHN 17:21 NLT

Jesus was the Son of God, but He still went to talk to His Father often in prayer. God wants you to do the same thing—give all your worries, fears, troubles, hopes, and requests to Him. And do it boldly! The Bible tells you not to be shy about asking for what you need (Hebrews 4:16). So pray big!

When you decide to follow Jesus, you are joined to the One who has all the answers, all the blessings, and everything you'll ever need. No matter what's happening around you or in your life, keep your focus on God. He's the One who saves, delivers, and heals you. He'll take care of you in ways you can't even imagine.

So pray. Talk to the Father, who knows all, controls all, has all the power, and is all-loving. He will help you.

*Lord Jesus, thank You for making me one with You and
giving me the amazing blessing of talking to God, amen.*

TODAY WITH JESUS . . . PRAY BOLDLY.

AUGUST 7

A FRIEND IN HIM

Come close to God, and God will come close to you.
JAMES 4:8 NLT

God, the Creator of the universe, wants to have a close relationship with you. But do you want to have a close relationship with Him?

God spoke to Moses "as a man speaks with his friend" (Exodus 33:11), and He wants to speak to you the same way. That happens when you spend time with Him. As you praise Him and tell Him how much you love Him, that's when God shows you who He is and how He loves you. Think about it this way: you may know a classmate's name, where he lives, and how good he is at math, but you won't really be friends until you spend time getting to know each other.

God wants you to get to know Him—how He works in your life, how He'll never leave you, and how He is the very best friend you'll ever have. And that takes time—time spent with Him.

*Lord, I want to know You. Please come closer
and show me who You are, amen.*

**TODAY WITH JESUS . . . SPEND TIME
GETTING TO KNOW GOD.**

GIFTS FOR YOU

A spiritual gift is given to each of us so we can help each other.
1 CORINTHIANS 12:7 NLT

God always has a plan. He doesn't just do *anything* without a good reason. For example, when He created the world, He created water *before* plants and animals because He knew they'd need something to drink. And when God created you, He also planned the work He wanted you to do—and gave you all the talents and gifts you'd need to do it.

What is it that God has planned for you? And what talents and gifts has He given you to carry out those plans? They're different for every person, but there is one thing that's certain: if you ask Him, He'll show you—maybe not His whole plan, but at least the next step in it.

Don't hide your gifts and talents—use them to serve Him. That not only blesses you, but it also praises Him. And it's what you were created for!

Father, thank You for the gifts You've given me.
Please show me how to use them for You, amen.

TODAY WITH JESUS . . . USE THE GIFTS HE'S GIVEN YOU.

WHY CHURCH?

You should not stay away from the church meetings, as some are doing. But you should meet together and encourage each other.
HEBREWS 10:25

Why is church important? After all, you can talk to God and read His Word anywhere. Well, church is important because that's where you'll find friendships with other believers, and a chance to worship, praise, and serve God together. You'll find encouragement in tough times and people who will teach you more about God. And, most important of all, you'll get a glimpse of how much the Lord loves you as His people love on you.

But maybe you had a bad experience at church. Someone hurt your feelings or you just don't feel like you fit in. Just remember, church isn't made up of perfect people. Instead, it's about worshipping a perfect God. You weren't created to go it alone. That's why God made the church—to gather His people together to love and help each other, and to give each other the strength and courage to get through each day (Galatians 6:2).

Lord, surround me with people who love You and who will help me love You even more, amen.

TODAY WITH JESUS . . . FIND A WAY TO HELP IN CHURCH.

DRAWING NEAR TO GOD

If I have truly pleased you, show me your plans. Then
I may know you and continue to please you.

EXODUS 33:13

Moses loved God. He didn't just believe the Lord was real—Moses wanted to live his life in a way that pleased God. So Moses prayed and tried to follow Him in everything he did and said. Because of that, God blessed Moses greatly (Exodus 33:19–23).

Let Moses be your example. Talk to God and read His Word to discover what pleases Him. Do those things in your life, and God will bless you too. As you come to understand how God thinks and works—though you'll never understand Him completely!—you'll be amazed by His great love and by the awesome ways He works in your life.

Knowing God changed Moses' life. It turned him from a runaway outlaw into the leader of all Israel. And knowing God will change your life, too—into a life that is complete, wonderful, never-ending, and full of the joy of God.

Lord, I want to understand how to live so that I can
please You. Please show me how, amen.

TODAY WITH JESUS . . . DISCOVER HIS WAYS.

DON'T BE STUBBORN

Humble yourself before the Lord, and he will honor you.
JAMES 4:10

It's important to spend time *meditating* on God—that means thinking about Him and His Word, and how it should change your life. But if you're stubborn and only interested in getting your own way, meditating will be very hard to do. Why? Because God will use your quiet time with Him to point out the things you need to change. And He'll keep on pointing them out until you agree with Him that they're an issue.

If you aren't willing to fix those things, you might be tempted to stop spending time with God—so you don't have to hear Him point out your sins. But that would be a huge mistake! Don't let sin and stubbornness keep you from getting close to God. Repent—agree that you're wrong and He's right. And enjoy spending time alone with God—the One who loves you so much that He'll tell you how to be free from the issues that are holding you back.

> *Lord, please show me the sins in my life. Help me*
> *to turn away from them and toward You, amen.*

TODAY WITH JESUS . . . MEDITATE ON GOD TODAY.

A GOD YOU CAN COUNT ON

*"Call to Me, and I will answer you, and show you great
and mighty things, which you do not know."*

JEREMIAH 33:3 NKJV

It's a fact: tough times and troubles just aren't fun, no matter who you are. Sooner or later, you'll wonder why those hard times have come into your life. You might even wonder if God still loves you. But the truth is, some of the greatest lessons you'll ever learn will come from the hardest of times. Why? Because it's during those times that you hold tightest to God—and you learn that you can count on Him.

When you go through troubles and tough times, it isn't because God wants to hurt you (Lamentations 3:32–33). Instead, God has things He wants to teach you—and some lessons can only be learned through struggles (Hebrews 5:8). And remember, God never leaves you alone in your troubles. He's right there beside you. So call on Him. And He'll teach you great and mighty things—things you need to know.

*Father, what do You want me to learn through my
troubles? Teach me, Lord. I am listening, amen.*

**TODAY WITH JESUS . . . TALK TO HIM—
AND EXPECT HIM TO ANSWER.**

LISTEN UP!

Listen, Israel, and carefully obey these laws.
Then all will go well for you.
DEUTERONOMY 6:3

What if God sent an actual letter—addressed *Dear (your name)* and signed *Love, God*—right to your mailbox? Would you stick it on the table and read it in a day or two? Of course not! You'd read it right away—over and over again! Why? Because you want to know what God has to say to you.

Well, you really do have a letter from God—the Bible. But so many believers just stick it on the table and never give a thought to what it says. And when they do read the Bible, they don't really *listen* to what it says. They don't let God's words sink into their hearts and change their lives.

But that doesn't have to be you. Read God's words and really listen to them. Think about them and let them change the way you live. Don't miss out on God's joy, love, and power—listen up! And learn all that your heavenly Father wants to show you.

> *Father, help me to really listen to Your words*
> *and let them change my life, amen.*

TODAY WITH JESUS . . . LET GOD'S WORDS CHANGE YOUR LIFE.

A PERFECT FIT

You are my Lord. Every good thing I have comes from you.

PSALM 16:2

You may have heard the old saying, "You can't put a square peg in a round hole"—it just won't fit. You need a round peg. In much the same way, you have a "hole" inside your heart that only God can fill. Some people try to fill it with other things—like popularity, money, or even drugs or alcohol—but none of them will work. Only God is a perfect fit.

When you reach out to God and ask Him to take up that place in your heart, He fills you up completely. He takes your focus off yourself and puts it on Jesus. And He begins transforming you—shaping you into the person He created you to be.

But none of that happens until you ask God to be Lord over every part of your life—not holding anything back. Give yourself to God, and let Him perfectly fill that hole in your heart.

Father, open up my heart and fill it with Your Spirit, amen.

TODAY WITH JESUS . . . OPEN YOUR HEART TO HIM.

DO IT HIS WAY

The Lord says, "Your thoughts are not like my
thoughts. Your ways are not like my ways."
ISAIAH 55:8

One day, God will ask you to do something that just doesn't make sense. For example, Jesus said that if someone smacks you on the cheek, don't hit back—offer him the other cheek instead (Matthew 5:39). That definitely doesn't make sense! Jesus also said if someone takes your coat, give him your shirt, too (Luke 6:29). He even said you should forgive those who hurt you (Matthew 6:14) and love those who hate you (Luke 6:27).

Jesus often did the exact opposite of what people expected Him to do. That's because He's not interested in being fair or getting even. He's interested in changing your heart and in showing His love to others through the things you do. You may not always understand what Jesus asks you to do, but you can believe it will always be best—and He'll bless you when you do things His way.

Father, help me do things Your way, even if
it doesn't make sense to me, amen.

TODAY WITH JESUS . . . BELIEVE HIS WAY IS BEST.

NO SHORTCUTS

"Whoever can be trusted with small things can also be trusted with large things."

LUKE 16:10

Today, you'll have a chance to take a shortcut and do less than your best—perhaps it's cleaning your room by shoving everything under the bed or finishing your homework by copying off a friend. You may have a million reasons for taking that shortcut, but is it worth throwing away a chance to please God—and to be rewarded by Him? Because God rewards those who choose to please Him.

Remember Joseph? He was sold into slavery, but he still worked hard for his master (Genesis 39:2). Even when he was thrown in prison, Joseph did his best (Genesis 39)—not just to please the prison warden, but to please God. And when the time was right, God blessed Joseph by making him second in command of all Egypt (Genesis 40–41).

Don't take shortcuts. Always give it your best, and God will bless you.

Lord, help me always to do my best—in big things and small—so that I will please You, amen.

TODAY WITH JESUS . . . DO YOUR BEST.

PRAISE HIM NOW!

It is good to praise the Lord, to sing praises to God Most High.
PSALM 92:1

When you talk to God—whether it's praising Him, telling Him about your day, or asking Him for something—do you talk with thanksgiving in your heart? Because when you come to God with praises, you are hurried right into His presence. Then you can go from worrying about your problems to worshipping the One who can solve them. And it's in those moments of love and adoration that God fills you with the peace of knowing He will take care of you.

So praise God—right now! Thank Him for His power to solve your problems, His wisdom to know what's best for you, and His mercy to forgive your sins. Praise Him for His love, for His perfect plan for your life, and for your future home in heaven. Don't wait—praise Him now!

God, You are my Savior, defender, guide, and friend.
Thank You for loving me so much, amen.

TODAY WITH JESUS . . . PRAISE HIM WITH ALL YOUR HEART.

CHOOSE TO FOLLOW HIM

"If anyone wants to follow me, he must say 'no' to the things he wants."
MATTHEW 16:24

Have you ever made a bad choice and then found yourself in a situation that isn't something God wants for you? Maybe you betrayed a friend and now you're dealing with her anger. Or you threw a fit and got thrown out of the game. Or you cheated on a test, and you're sitting in the principal's office, wondering what's going to happen next.

Dear child, God is always ready to help you and guide you—even out of the worst situations. But He won't do it until you admit you were wrong and you're willing to do what He says. Think about it: Jesus was always there for His disciples, but they had to *choose* to follow and obey Him. He never forced anyone to follow Him, but those who did were changed forever.

You have the same choice today. *Choose* to follow and obey Him—and He'll change your life forever.

*Father, I choose to follow You. Please help me
to follow wherever You lead, amen.*

TODAY WITH JESUS . . . CHOOSE HIM.

DO NOT BE SHAKEN

*I keep the Lord before me always. Because he
is close by my side I will not be hurt.*
PSALM 16:8

The angel Gabriel told Mary she would have a baby—even though she wasn't married—and she was willing to risk the shame. Paul was beaten and thrown in prison, but he wouldn't stop teaching about Jesus. King Saul tried to kill David, but David still praised God.

How were these people able to do such things? Because they trusted God completely, and they knew His love for them would never change or end. God's presence with them helped them stay faithful—even when times got very hard.

As you spend time with God, you'll learn to trust Him completely, too. When you understand He uses His mighty power to help you, you won't be afraid. When you understand His love never ends, you'll find the strength to keep going. And when you see He takes care of you—no matter what—then your faith will not be shaken.

*Father, help me to keep learning more and more about
You, so that my faith will not be shaken, amen.*

**TODAY WITH JESUS . . . READ ABOUT
MARY'S GREAT FAITH IN LUKE 1:38.**

LET GOD GUIDE YOU

This lesson comes from the Lord of heaven's armies.
He gives wonderful advice. He is very wise.

ISAIAH 28:29

Do you trust God to lead you in the way that's absolutely best for you? A lot of people say they trust God, but their actions tell a *completely* different story.

Sometimes the advice of other people gets in the way. For example, your friend said something hurtful, and you know God wants you to forgive—but another friend whispers the perfect comeback or encourages you to plot revenge. At other times, it's your own pride that keeps you from obeying God. For example, perhaps you know that argument was your fault and you need to apologize, but you just don't want to admit you're wrong. But remember, refusing to obey God will only lead to more hurt and trouble.

Only God has perfect knowledge—not your friends and not your pride. Only God can guide you perfectly. Listen to Him, and obey Him—each and every time.

Lord, teach me to turn to You first—not to
my friends or even to myself, amen.

TODAY WITH JESUS . . . BELIEVE HIS WAY IS BEST.

AUGUST 21

IN TRAINING

"Before I made you in your mother's womb, I chose you. Before you were born, I set you apart for a special work."
JEREMIAH 1:5

Do you ever feel like asking, "God, I'm just a kid, can You really use me?" The answer is yes, He can! No matter how old or young you are, God has amazing plans for you. And He's training you for those plans—right this very moment.

How can you know for sure? Because when you decide to follow God, you become His own beloved child. And because of that, He'll work through you—not using just your strength, intelligence, and talents, but adding His power, wisdom, and abilities to yours. With God's help and training, you'll be able to do all the good works He has planned for you—plans He made before you were even born.

God will bless you, but He'll allow some troubles into your life too. They're part of your training—teaching you to depend on Him and follow Him, because He'll never let you down when you do.

Father, thank You for training me and guiding me through Your plans for my life, amen.

TODAY WITH JESUS . . . DISCOVER WHAT HE CAN DO THROUGH YOU.

THE RIGHT REASONS

All who follow my ways are joyful.
PROVERBS 8:32 NLT

God is *always* teaching you—in the big, amazing moments of your life and in the ordinary, everyday moments. He wants you to learn how big and mighty and holy He is. But He also wants you to understand that He is loving, good, and kind. And He wants you to learn to be just like Him—loving, good, and kind too.

That means God wants you to help and serve people, but for the right reasons. Not to show off, not to look good, and not just because it's something you're supposed to do. God wants you to help and serve because you love people and want what's best for them—just as He does. Because it is what He created you to do.

You see, when God is working in your life, He helps you see the world through His eyes and love its people with His heart. He inspires you to reach out to others, and He fills you with His strength and heavenly peace. It is then you can become all He created you to be and find real joy.

Lord, please help me see with Your eyes
and love with Your heart, amen.

TODAY WITH JESUS . . . HELP SOMEONE.

NO REGRETS

*I will listen to God the Lord. He has ordered
peace for his people who worship him.*
PSALM 85:8

Regrets. Everyone has them. You wish you hadn't said what you said or done what you did. But there's one thing you'll never, ever regret—and that's obeying God. But sadly, that's the one thing so many people refuse to do.

People lie, cheat, and steal—even though God said not to—and then they're afraid of getting caught. They argue with their parents and disrespect their teachers, then fear the trouble they know is coming. They refuse to do chores or homework, and then worry about the price they'll pay. They keep on pretending that their way is the easy way, but it's not. It always ends up much, much harder than if they'd just obeyed God in the first place.

When you ask God to help you obey Him, He does that and more. He transforms you, so that you actually want the things He wants. And then you'll have no regrets.

*Jesus, please help me to want the things You want
and obey You so that I have no regrets, amen.*

TODAY WITH JESUS . . . DO WHAT HE WANTS YOU TO DO.

CLING TO HIM

The Lord is my shepherd. I have everything I need.
PSALM 23:1

S ometimes God's way of doing things can be confusing. Part of the confusion is because He's God and He's simply too big to understand. But another part comes from the fact that you'd rather not have any troubles, sadness, or disappointments in your life. And if a problem does pop up, you'd like it to be fixed pretty quickly.

And *that's* when the Devil attacks. When a problem doesn't go away, when sad times strike, when disappointments pile up, the Devil whispers his lies and asks if God really *does* know what's best for you. Don't listen to him!

The Devil only wants to hurt you and pull you away from God. But God loves you and will use everything in your life to teach, help, and shape you to be more like Jesus. Hold tight to Him, and He'll protect you from the Devil's lies. Because He really does want what's best for you.

Lord, protect me from the lies of the Devil. I will
trust You to do what's best for me, amen.

**TODAY WITH JESUS . . . LISTEN TO
GOD, NOT THE DEVIL'S LIES.**

SEARCH FOR HIM

*My soul wants to be with you at night. And my spirit
wants to be with you at the dawn of every day.*
ISAIAH 26:9

You *want* to spend more time with God. You plan out exactly *when* you're going to do it. But it never quite seems to work out. Then, before you know it, it's time for bed—and you still haven't talked to God or read your Bible.

God commands you to search for Him—to get to know Him and His ways. And He promises that if you seek Him, you'll find Him. But that searching won't just happen by accident—you have to put God first. Don't make excuses about homework, chores, or practice. Don't say you're too busy or too tired. Don't let anything keep you away from God. Search for Him, and He'll show you who He is and how much He loves you. Seek God every single day—and then, when the hard times come, you'll know exactly where to find Him.

> *Lord, help me take time to be with You
> each and every day, amen.*

TODAY WITH JESUS . . . PUT GOD FIRST.

SIMPLY BE WITH GOD

"Martha, Martha, you are getting worried and upset about too many things. Only one thing is important."

LUKE 10:41–42

Martha hurried from one thing to the next, preparing dinner for Jesus and the disciples—while her sister, Mary, just sat, listening to Jesus. The more Martha hurried, the angrier she got. Finally, she'd had enough: "Lord . . . tell her to help me!" (Luke 10:40). But Jesus didn't fuss at Mary. Instead, He gently scolded Martha. Yes, Martha's work was important—after all, she was trying to serve Jesus. But it wasn't as important as simply *being* with God.

Do you ever get so busy with school, chores, practices, family, and friends—even serving God—that you forget to simply *be* with God? Reading God's Word, praying, and praising Him are very important, but so is simply being still and quiet with Him. Because that's when He pulls you close, holds you, and whispers how much He loves you.

Lord, I'm so thankful that I can come and sit with You anytime. Hold me and draw me closer to You, amen.

TODAY WITH JESUS . . . BE STILL WITH HIM.

A LITTLE BIT OF HEAVEN

You are worthy to take the scroll . . . because you were
killed; and with the blood of your death you bought men for
God from every tribe, language, people, and nation.
REVELATION 5:9

Do you wish you could get just a peek into heaven? To see its wonders? God gave the apostle John a peek into heaven. He saw the wonder of it all. But what most amazed John was how much he wanted to just stop and praise Jesus. And he wasn't alone. Heaven was filled with angels, living creatures, and elders saying, "All praise and honor and glory and power forever and ever to . . . the Lamb!" (Revelation 5:13).

One day, you'll stand before Jesus. And on that day, everything else will seem so unimportant—even the troubles that seem so huge today. Your heart will be filled with a longing to bow down and worship Him. But you don't have to wait for that day—bow down and worship Him right now. And that time in His presence will bring a little bit of heaven down to earth.

> *Jesus, thank You for saving me and for being*
> *so good to me. I praise You, Lord! Amen.*

TODAY WITH JESUS . . . WORSHIP HIM.

NONE LIKE HIM

*The Lord gives strength to his people. The
Lord blesses his people with peace.*

PSALM 29:11

S ome people don't want to get close to God because they're afraid
He'll ask them to do something hard, or give up something they
don't want to give up. They think any troubles they have are because
God doesn't care or He's punishing them. But once they decide to
trust Him, they stop worrying about those things. Why? Because
they know they can trust God—and that He only wants the absolute
best for them.

God is God. There is no one else like Him. He may allow hard
times to come into your life to point out a sin you need to get rid of, or
to teach you that you really can count on Him. God understands that
if you never had a single problem, then you'd also never know one of
life's greatest joys—the joy of watching Him work in your life when
you need Him most.

*Lord, thank You for loving, teaching, protecting, and
taking care of me. You are so good, amen.*

TODAY WITH JESUS . . . KNOW THAT HE IS GOOD.

AT A CROSSROADS

Happy is the person who trusts the Lord.
PSALM 40:4

A *crossroads* is the point where two roads meet, and you have to choose which way to go. One day—and it may already have happened—you'll come to a crossroads in your faith. It's where you'll have to choose: *Do I really trust God? Do I really believe He'll help me, or are those just words I say?*

God understands that trusting Him is hard sometimes. He knows it takes time and practice. But He also knows you can learn to trust Him completely—with His help.

You may not understand God's ways. After all, they're so much bigger and greater than your human ways (Isaiah 55:8). But you can know that when you follow Him, His Holy Spirit will come and live inside you to guide you every inch of the way (John 16:13). So choose the road that leads to trusting Him—and He'll bless you in ways you never even imagined.

God, thank You for Your Holy Spirit, who guides
me and helps me follow Your ways, amen.

TODAY WITH JESUS . . . PRACTICE TRUSTING HIM.

DECIDE NOW

For the good of your name, lead me and guide me.

PSALM 31:3

Every second of your life, God is looking out for you. He *always* has your best interests at heart. There's never a moment that He gets tired of you, or stops loving you, or stops working to take care of you. He promises to guide you on the very best path for your life if you'll follow Him (Psalm 16:11; 32:8).

You can only see what's happening right this very second, but God can see yesterday, today, and tomorrow. So why wouldn't you ask Him to show you the way? And not just in the big choices and decisions, but in all the everyday ones too.

Do you *ask* God to guide you? Do you let His Holy Spirit show you the way to go? Or do you *tell* God how you want things to go? Decide now that you'll trust God—and let Him lead you in the way that's best for you.

God, I want You to guide all my choices—
no matter how big or small, amen.

TODAY WITH JESUS . . . ASK HIM
ABOUT ALL YOUR DECISIONS.

LOVE THROUGH FORGIVENESS

"I tell you, her sins—and they are many—have been forgiven, so she has shown me much love."
LUKE 7:47 NLT

Some people never know the wonderful richness of God's love. Maybe it's because they don't choose to believe He's real, or they don't trust Him. But it could be because they refuse to forgive.

Is there someone you're refusing to forgive? Maybe it's someone who never apologized, or someone who hurt you so badly you don't think he or she *deserves* to be forgiven. But that attitude only hurts you. You see, Jesus died on the cross so that you could be forgiven, because that's how much He loves you. But when you refuse to forgive others, it builds up a wall between you and God, and that hinders you from experiencing an awesome relationship with Him.

Forgive others the way God wants to forgive to you. Then there will be no wall—and you'll be blessed with the wonderful riches of God's amazing love.

Jesus, please give me the strength to forgive those who've hurt me, amen.

TODAY WITH JESUS . . . CHOOSE TO FORGIVE.

SEPTEMBER

LET IT GO!

*If we confess our sins, he will forgive our sins. . . . He will
make us clean from all the wrongs we have done.*
1 JOHN 1:9

You goofed. You messed up. You knew it was the wrong thing to
say, the wrong thing to do. And now you feel so ashamed. You just
want to hide away from the whole world—even from God. It all happened days, weeks, or even months ago, but those horrible feelings
just won't go away.

Dear child, God does not want you to live with that kind of shame.
When He forgives you, He also takes away all the reasons you feel
unworthy or embarrassed (Psalm 103:12). That sin is washed away.
You are clean, loved, and cherished by God.

Don't get stuck in the past. Don't let your mistakes keep you from
the amazing future God has planned for you. Ask God to forgive you.
And then forgive yourself. Remind yourself who you really are—a
forgiven, cleansed, and beloved child of God. And all that shame?
Just let it go!

*Lord Jesus, thank You for forgiving me. Help me to
forgive myself and let go of the shame, amen.*

TODAY WITH JESUS . . . LET HIM MAKE YOU CLEAN.

WHEN GOD SAYS NO

To me, living means living for Christ.
PHILIPPIANS 1:21 NLT

You prayed and prayed, and God did answer—but it wasn't the answer you wanted. So . . . what do you do now? Do you get angry with God because you didn't get your way? Do you start to doubt that He really wants what's best for you? Do you wonder if He still loves you? Or do you say, "I don't understand this, God, but I still trust You. I know You only do what's best for me."

What you do when God says no says a lot about you—whether you are self-centered or God-centered, whether you are more interested in what you want or what God wants.

If your answers show that you still have some work to do, don't be surprised or upset. After all, God's still working on you. He's teaching you to trust Him completely, *especially* when He says no.

God, forgive me for the times I think only about what
I want. Help me to want what You want, amen.

TODAY WITH JESUS . . . FOCUS ON WHAT PLEASES HIM.

DON'T WORRY

"Do not worry about your life."
MATTHEW 6:25 NIV

Do you worry . . . *a lot*? Do you wake up afraid of what might happen that day, and then go to bed stressed over what did or didn't happen? Fear happens when you try to face life on your own—without asking God for His help, power, courage, and strength.

You see, God will never force you to seek Him. He gives you free will, which means you must *choose* to come to Him for help. But if you choose to avoid Him, He may allow some troubles to come into your life to remind you that you need Him.

If you find yourself worried and afraid, that's a pretty good sign that you need to talk to God. Go to Him in prayer and in His Word. He's your loving Father, and He doesn't want you to live in fear. Seek Him, trust Him, and give all your worries to Him.

*Father, I will not worry or be afraid, because I
know You are with me always, amen.*

TODAY WITH JESUS . . . GIVE HIM YOUR WORRIES.

GOD WILL SHOW YOU

"Keep on asking, and you will receive what you ask for. Keep on seeking, and you will find. Keep on knocking, and the door will be opened to you."

MATTHEW 7:7 NLT

Would your mom tell you to make your bed without ever showing you how? Would your dad tell you to take out the trash but never tell you where the garbage can was kept? Or would a teacher give you a huge math problem but refuse to explain how to do it? Of course not!

In the same way, God would never tell you to obey Him without showing you how (Matthew 7:11). When you ask God what you should do, He *will* tell you. He may answer through His Word, through another person, or in a completely different way. Also, He may show you only the next step, when you'd really rather know the whole plan. Regardless, God will reveal exactly what you need to know.

The point is, talk to God and trust Him. He'll show you what to do. Ask Him to help you and then listen for His answer—because it's coming and it will be the perfect path for you to follow.

Lord, You know what is best for me. Show me what I need to do, amen.

TODAY WITH JESUS . . . KNOW THAT GOD WILL ANSWER YOU.

OBEY ANYWAY

*Simon answered, "Master, we worked hard all night
trying to catch fish, but we caught nothing. But you
say to put the nets in the water; so I will."*
LUKE 5:5

God's ways of doing things are often very different from yours, which means that His plans for your life—and even for today—will probably be different from yours (Isaiah 55:8–9).

Think about Peter. He fished all night and didn't catch a thing. So when Jesus told him to go and fish some more, Peter didn't think that was such a great idea. After all, he was tired, he'd just cleaned his nets, and Jesus wasn't a professional fisherman like he was. But Peter obeyed anyway—and he caught so many fish his nets almost broke (Luke 5:1–11)! Obeying Jesus changed Peter's life forever, and from that day on, Peter followed Him.

Obeying Jesus will change your life forever, too. Do what He says—even if it doesn't make sense. Because when you do things His way, amazing things happen. And you don't want to miss a single one!

Lord, I will obey You, even when I don't understand, amen.

TODAY WITH JESUS . . . DO WHAT HIS WORD SAYS.

DECIDE TO OBEY

"Come to me and listen. Listen to me so you may live."

ISAIAH 55:3

Today, before you pray and before you read God's Word, decide that you will do what He says. God may challenge you—asking you to do hard things. But He always has a good reason for everything He tells you to do—whether it is getting rid of a sinful habit or making your faith in Him grow stronger. You can be absolutely certain He wants what's best for you. So don't be surprised if obeying Him isn't easy. But decide now to obey Him anyway.

Friend, God understands that becoming the person He created you to be is difficult. But it is supposed to stretch you so you'll depend on Him. You may not always understand why God asks you to do something, but you can be sure that He'll bless you if you obey Him. So ask Him and He will help you. He will give you the courage and strength you need because He wants you to succeed and to experience life at its very best.

Lord, today I choose to obey You—no matter what, amen.

TODAY WITH JESUS . . . DECIDE TO OBEY HIM.

DON'T JUST JUMP IN

*Those who plan and work hard earn a profit. But
those who act too quickly become poor.*
PROVERBS 21:5

There will be times when you're tempted to just jump in and make a decision—without talking to God first. And Satan will be right there, whispering, "Go ahead! This is easy. Don't bother God with this. You'll be fine!" But that sneaky snake never mentions what happens *after* the decision, because what he really wants is to tear you down and destroy you.

But God cares—about you, your decisions, and what happens after those decisions. God wants only the best for you.

Remember, God isn't just the God of today—He's also the God of the future. He's the perfect guide for your decisions, and He wants you to ask, "If I choose this, what will happen—to me, my family, my friendships? Will this choice please You or pull me away from You?" Ask God to guide you—and He'll make sure your future is bright (Jeremiah 29:11).

> *Lord, You know everything—even the future. So
> please guide me to what You know is best, amen.*

HIS PEACE

God's peace will keep your hearts and minds in Christ Jesus. The peace that God gives is so great that we cannot understand it.

PHILIPPIANS 4:7

When you first start to pray, peace probably isn't what you're feeling. You may be feeling anger, worry, stress, fear, or sadness instead. But when God speaks to you, one of the first things you'll notice is a sense of peace. And the longer you talk to God and listen to Him, the quieter your spirit will become. You'll experience that peace "so great that [you] cannot understand it."

This is what God's presence and guidance give you—confidence and assurance. Of course, if you don't obey God, you won't have peace—no matter how long you pray. For example, you can't lie and expect God to bless you. You'll have to get rid of that sin first.

But when God speaks and you agree to obey Him, you'll know without a doubt that it's the right thing to do because His peace will fill you. You become confident because you know that whatever God says, He will do.

Father God, help me to obey You so that I can be filled with Your peace, amen.

TODAY WITH JESUS . . . LET GOD FILL YOU WITH HIS PEACE.

WHAT "MEDITATION" MEANS

King David went in and sat before the Lord and prayed.
2 SAMUEL 7:18 NLT

Look at today's verse: "David . . . sat before the Lord." That means David was *meditating*—thinking about God. This was a perfectly natural thing for David to do. After all, David was a man after God's own heart, so he wanted to know God's plan for his life. And often, it was when David was meditating that God showed him that plan—or at least the next step of it.

Meditating, or thinking about God, is something you should do every day too. Of course, Satan will try everything he can think of to stop you. He'll tell you that you're too busy, and it's not that important anyway. He'll distract you with hobbies, movies, or friends. But don't let him. That time spent with God is priceless!

If you have a problem, a choice to make, or just want to listen to God, meditate on Him—and He'll certainly be with you.

*Lord, help me take time to meditate on You. It's
the most important part of my day, amen.*

TODAY WITH JESUS . . . THINK ABOUT HIM.

LIVE IN PEACE

Stop doing evil and do good. Look for peace and work for it.
PSALM 34:14

The Bible says, "Try to live in peace with all people" (Hebrews 12:14). That doesn't mean doing things you know are wrong just to keep the peace. But it *does* mean being kind and loving to all people, praying for God to guide you, and being willing to forgive others.

One way to "live in peace" is to ask God to help you understand where other people are coming from. For example, if your best friend suddenly snaps at you, of course it hurts. But when you later find out she'd just gotten some really bad news about her grandmother, you understand why she wasn't her usual friendly self.

To live in peace, you'll need God's help to understand who other people really are and what burdens they're carrying (1 John 4:20). So ask Him to help you see with His eyes and love with His heart—that's the surest way to peace.

Lord, help me always be loving and kind—
to live in peace with everyone, amen.

TODAY WITH JESUS . . . ASK HIM TO
HELP YOU SEE WITH HIS EYES.

DON'T STRIKE BACK!

"People will insult you and hurt you . . . because you follow me. But when they do, you will be blessed."
MATTHEW 5:11 NCV

It's no fun being laughed at or bullied. In fact, it hurts—a lot. But the fact is, when you follow Jesus, there will be people who will attack you because of it. They'll laugh at you, bully you, or worse. You'll be tempted to get even, but don't—let God take care of that. Instead, do good to those who attack you, pray for them, and forgive them. Why? Because they're caught up in the Devil's trap, and showing them God's love might be very thing that sets them free (2 Timothy 2:26).

Of course, this won't be easy. You'll need to ask God for His strength to do it. And you'll need to trust Him to get you through the hard times. But when others attack you for believing in Jesus, don't give up and don't strike back. Rejoice instead—because then you get to show everyone just how great and loving your God is.

Lord, when others are mean, help me to forgive and to be kind, amen.

TODAY WITH JESUS . . . FORGIVE THOSE WHO ATTACK YOU.

BECAUSE YOU'RE FORGIVEN

"If you forgive others for the things they do wrong, then your Father in heaven will also forgive you for the things you do wrong."

MATTHEW 6:14

Have you ever had your feelings hurt by a friend? You might want to just stop being friends or even hurt her back. Choose to forgive instead. Why? Because if you don't, your hurt feelings can easily turn into anger and bitterness—and that's never a good thing.

Of course, the absolute worst thing about not forgiving others is that it pulls you away from God. Jesus died on the cross so that you could be forgiven. And in return, He asks that you forgive others. You simply can't expect God to forgive you, if you won't forgive others.

So be kind to the one who hurt you—just as Jesus is kind and loving to you. Ask Him to fix your relationship with that person and your relationship with Him. When you choose to forgive, you'll begin to understand all that Jesus did on the cross so that He could forgive you.

Father, help me to forgive those who hurt me
and to show them Your love, amen.

TODAY WITH JESUS . . . BE AS FORGIVING AS JESUS.

FEAR OF THE LORD

Fear of the LORD is the foundation of true knowledge.
PROVERBS 1:7 NLT

The words "fear of the LORD" can be a bit confusing. This kind of fear isn't about being frightened or afraid. Instead, it means to respect and to be in awe of God because you understand that He is Lord of all creation and is perfect and holy in every way.

God doesn't want you to be afraid of Him. He wants you to know how great His love for you is, and that He'll always do what's best for you. But He also expects you to obey Him. And sometimes the things He asks you to do may be frightening—like telling others about Him, reaching out to help someone, or standing up for what's right. It's your "fear of the LORD"—your respect for Him—that will give you the courage to obey Him.

Today, let your "fear of the LORD" help you overcome your earthly fears so that you can obey Him.

Father, You are perfect and holy and all-powerful. Help me to obey You, amen.

ARE YOU LISTENING?

Who among you fears the Lord and obeys his servant? . . .
Let him trust in the Lord. Let him depend on his God.

ISAIAH 50:10

God is always talking to you—through His Word, through the words of other people, and through the things that happen in your life. But are you listening?

God's voice begins as a whisper, so you must listen carefully. If you aren't listening, He'll get louder. No, you probably won't hear a big, booming voice from heaven calling out your name. But God will allow people and events into your life—even troubles—to get your attention.

Don't force God to "shout" at you. Read His Word—every day—so you can know Him and what He wants from you. He wants to guide (Psalm 48:14), comfort, (2 Corinthians 1:3), and protect you (Genesis 19:17–26). He wants to teach you to obey Him (Joshua 6:18–19) and to show you how much He loves you (John 16:27). Don't let the noise of this world drown Him out. Listen to God!

Lord, open my ears to hear everything
You are saying to me, amen.

TODAY WITH JESUS . . . LISTEN TO HIM.

A HEALTHY BODY

You are joined together with peace through the Spirit. Do all you can to continue together in this way. Let peace hold you together.
EPHESIANS 4:3

Your body is amazing! All the different parts work together in ways scientists still don't completely understand. Just think about all that happens as you read this page: your eyes see the words and send an image to your brain, which then translates it into a message you can understand. And all the while, you're breathing, blinking, turning the page, and maybe fidgeting in your chair. When something goes wrong with part of your body, your whole body is affected—like stubbing your toe makes your eyes water and your teeth clench.

The body of Christ—the church—works a lot like your body. Every part, or person, is important. When one person hurts, the entire body suffers. That's why God challenges you to "be kind and loving to each other" (Ephesians 4:32) and to forgive, help, and encourage one another (Hebrews 3:13). That's how you can help keep the church body healthy and strong!

> *Father, help me to see those who are hurting and to reach out to them with Your love, amen.*

TODAY WITH JESUS . . . DO SOMETHING KIND FOR SOMEONE IN YOUR CHURCH.

WIN AGAINST THE WORLD

Everyone who is a child of God has the power to win against the world. It is our faith that wins the victory against the world.

1 JOHN 5:4

Sometimes life is just hard. There's sickness and sadness. Friends move away or betray you. You flunk a test, strike out, or don't make the team. Because sin is part of this world, tough times are also part of this world. But it's what you do with those challenging times that really matters. Do you fall apart, get angry, or just give up? Or do you trust God to get you through?

When you're are a child of God, He promises to use everything in your life—even the hard stuff—for your good and for His glory. It's difficult to remember His promises when you're in the middle of one of those tough times. That's why it's so important to turn to God. Ask Him to remind you of His promises and fill you with His strength and hope. No matter how bad things look, God will help you win against this world!

*Lord, when life is tough, help me to hold
even tighter to You, amen.*

**TODAY WITH JESUS . . . TRUST HIM
TO GET YOU THROUGH.**

FAILING FOR A REASON

My honor and salvation come from God. He is
my mighty rock and my protection.
PSALM 62:7

If I mess this up, what will everybody think? That's exactly the kind of thinking that can fill you with worry and fear. But here's something else to think about: what if God put failure in your life for a reason—to teach you to trust Him?

Of course, your failure could be because of a sin God wants you to get rid of. But it could also be that God is trying to teach you to depend on Him. These kinds of lessons aren't fun—after all, you're human and you like to succeed. The trouble is that, so often, you like to succeed all on your own. You leave God out—and that's when He'll use disappointments to remind you that you really do need Him. But as you learn to trust Him more and more, you'll see those failures are just steps on your way to a bigger victory in Him.

Lord, help me trust You completely—
especially when I fail, amen.

TODAY WITH JESUS . . . DEPEND ON HIM ALL THE TIME.

THE BLAME GAME

People are tempted when their own evil desire
leads them away and traps them.

JAMES 1:14 NCV

When God asked Adam if he'd eaten the forbidden fruit, Adam did what a lot of people today still do: he blamed someone else (Genesis 3:12). Instead of admitting he was wrong, Adam said it was Eve's fault. Do you ever blame someone else, instead of admitting that *you're* wrong?

Blaming someone else is an easy thing to do. After all, you don't want to get into trouble, so it's tempting to blame whoever is nearby. But God doesn't want you to take the easy way out—and it won't work anyway. You might be able to fool your friends, teachers, or even parents (although that's not a good idea either!), but you'll never deceive God. He already knows exactly what you've done.

So don't play the blame game. Admit to God that you've sinned. He's just waiting to forgive you and help you make things right again.

Lord, thank You for being a God I can come to when I sin—a
God who will forgive me and love me always, amen.

TODAY WITH JESUS . . . DON'T PLAY THE BLAME GAME.

SEPTEMBER 19

FORGIVE LIKE JESUS

Be kind and loving to each other. Forgive each
other just as God forgave you in Christ.
EPHESIANS 4:32

There will always be someone you need to forgive. It might be a classmate who talks about you behind your back, a friend who lets you down, a teacher who accuses you of cheating when you didn't, or someone who just made you feel unimportant. Forgiving isn't easy, but it is necessary. And the longer you wait to forgive, the more bitter you'll become and the harder it will be.

Why should you forgive? Because Jesus forgives you. When you decide to follow Him, Jesus washes away your every sin—because He loves you. Show Jesus how much you love Him, too, by forgiving those who wrong you.

You should also forgive because the one hurt most by your unforgiveness is . . . *you*. It fills your heart with anger and bitterness, and that's not the life Jesus wants for you. If you want to be more like Jesus, then forgive others just as He forgave you.

Lord, give me the courage to let go of my anger
and forgive those who've hurt me, amen.

TODAY WITH JESUS . . . FORGIVE OTHERS.

PERFECT PERFECTION

God is strong and can help you not to fall. He can bring you before his glory without any wrong in you and give you great joy.

JUDE V. 24

Are you trying to be perfect? The perfect student, perfect daughter or son, perfect friend, perfect player—even the perfect child of God? Have you figured out yet that it's not possible to be perfect?

The good news is you don't have to be perfect for God. Read and remember these truths: No one can do what it is right all the time. No one can be completely free of sin—except Jesus. And Jesus has washed away all your sins. You aren't perfect, but you are blameless because of Him. Let that give you great joy!

You live in a world full of sin, so you'll be tempted to do bad things and sometimes you'll make wrong decisions. In other words, you won't be perfect. But when you follow Jesus, you are covered with His perfection—so that when God looks at you, He sees the strength, goodness, and perfection of Jesus. And *that* is perfect salvation.

Dear God, thank You for Your perfect Son who takes away all my sins and mistakes, amen.

TODAY WITH JESUS . . . BELIEVE YOU ARE BLAMELESS BECAUSE OF HIM.

LISTEN FOR HIS VOICE

If a person's thinking is controlled by his sinful self,
then there is death. But if his thinking is controlled
by the Spirit, then there is life and peace.
ROMANS 8:6

God will never tell you to just do whatever you want. And He'll never tell you to do whatever makes you happy without thinking about the future. Yes, He wants you to enjoy this life He's given you. But He wants you to experience it in a way that both pleases Him and is good for you—not in a way that will end up hurting you.

So be careful and be wise. There are lots of voices in this world that will tell you to do whatever feels good—whether it's gossip or lying, shoplifting, drugs or alcohol. Don't listen to those voices. Listen to the voice of God. Ask His Holy Spirit to guide you away from hurtful things—especially those destructive things that disguise themselves as quick and easy fun.

Fill your mind with thoughts of God and His Word. Listen for His voice—and follow Him to a beautiful life.

Lord, help me hear Your voice above all
others and follow You, amen.

TODAY WITH JESUS . . . LISTEN FOR HIS VOICE.

GOD NEVER BREAKS A PROMISE

The Lord has kept all the good promises he gave.

1 KINGS 8:56

People may break their promises, but not God. He *always* keeps His promises. Every single one of them. So if He has given you a promise, you can believe He will fulfill it. It may not happen exactly when you want it to or the way you want it to, but it will be perfect for you.

So many people start to doubt God because they don't see Him working in their lives the way they think He should. They start out praying and believing God will answer, but when nothing changes right away, they give up on God.

If you're praying and waiting for God to answer, have courage and keep believing that He is acting on your behalf. If He asks you to wait, that's because He's busy working everything out in a way that's too wonderful for words. Trust God—He's never broken a promise and He never will.

Dear God, I know You always keep Your promises. Help me remember that when I'm waiting for You to answer, amen.

TODAY WITH JESUS . . . BELIEVE HE'LL KEEP HIS PROMISES.

IMPOSSIBLE THINGS

Oh, Lord God, you made the skies and the earth. You made them with your very great power. There is nothing too wonderful for you to do.
JEREMIAH 32:17

King Herod did not like the followers of Jesus. He hated them so much that he had the apostle Peter arrested and chained in prison. The people of the church prayed and prayed for Peter, but saving him seemed impossible. But then, the night before Peter's trial, the impossible happened.

Peter was sleeping, when an angel of the Lord suddenly appeared and said, "Get up!" Peter's chains fell away. He stood and walked past all the guards—they never even saw him. He walked right out of the prison and down the street to where his friends were still gathered, praying for him. At first, the people didn't believe Peter had escaped, but then they realized God had answered their prayers. He had made the impossible possible (Acts 12).

God can do anything. Absolutely nothing is too hard for Him. So when things in your life looks impossible, trust God. He makes the impossible . . . possible.

Dear God, You made the universe and everything
in it. Nothing is too hard for You, amen.

TODAY WITH JESUS . . . BELIEVE HE
CAN DO IMPOSSIBLE THINGS.

SWEET PEACE

Many are against me. But he keeps me safe in battle.

PSALM 55:18

When do you feel most peaceful? Is it early in the morning, when it's still and quiet? Or perhaps it's at night, just before you fall asleep. Maybe you have a special spot—under a tree or in your favorite chair—that helps you feel safe and secure. That kind of peace is wonderful, but it's worldly peace that depends on a time and a place. There's another kind of peace that you can have no matter where you are or what's around you: the peace of God.

Peace means to "bind together" something that's been broken. When worries, troubles, and dramas seem to tear you apart, go to God. He'll "bind you together" and seal you with His peace. He'll quiet the worried whispers of your mind and give your weary heart rest. He'll brush away trouble and remind you of how much you're loved. Go to God—and be wrapped in His sweet peace.

Lord, thank You for Your peace. All my worries
fade away when I come to You, amen.

TODAY WITH JESUS . . . GO TO HIM EVERY DAY.

HE'LL TEACH YOU THE WAY

See if there is any bad thing in me. Lead me
on the road to everlasting life.
PSALM 139:24 NCV

When you ask God what you should do, do you ever have trouble understanding what He wants? If so, pray and ask Him to show you verses from the Bible—promises that you can hold on to until you're sure of what He wants you to do.

Don't just rush ahead and do whatever you think is right. Instead, take time to open up the Bible and ask God for verses to help you understand what He desires from you. These verses will anchor you to Him and keep you from drifting away—just as a boat anchor keeps a boat from drifting away.

And if you still don't get what He wants, keep asking. Because God *wants* you to understand what He expects from you, so He'll keep showing and explaining until you comprehend His instructions. Trust Him to teach you the way.

Lord, show me the verses that will teach me
what You want me to do, amen.

TODAY WITH JESUS . . . TRUST HIM TO TEACH YOU.

A JOB FOR YOU

Christ carried our sins in his body on the cross. He did this
so that we would stop living for sin and start living for what
is right. And we are healed because of his wounds.

1 PETER 2:24

Jesus has a job for you: tell everyone the good news of salvation—that He purchased forgiveness from sin for all of us on the cross (Matthew 28:19). That *sounds* easy. After all, Jesus' gift to us is so amazing, why wouldn't you tell everyone about it?

But what if . . . you meet someone who doesn't believe in God or makes fun of people who do believe? Or you meet someone so sinful that you think there's no point in telling him about Jesus? That's when you need to remember Jesus' own words: "Healthy people don't need a doctor. It is the sick who need a doctor. I did not come to invite good people. I came to invite sinners" (Mark 2:17).

The more sin a person has in his life, the more that person needs to hear about Jesus. And Jesus is hoping that you'll be the one to share His good news.

Dear God, show me someone I can tell about You today—
and help me be brave enough to do it, amen.

TODAY WITH JESUS . . . SHOW HIS
LOVE TO EVERYONE YOU MEET.

A GOOD LOSER

He holds success in store for the upright.
PROVERBS 2:7 NIV

If you play games or sports, you know it's important to be a good loser. And what does being a good loser look like? You don't throw a fit or beat yourself up; instead, you learn how you can be better next time.

Well, losing can happen in almost any part of your life—not just sports and games. Maybe you tried to do the right thing, but it didn't work out. Or you *thought* you were going in the right direction, but it turned out all wrong. It's still important to be a good loser. Don't beat yourself up or throw a fit. Instead, look for the lessons God can teach you—so you can do better next time.

For example, you might learn you can't do some things on your own—but you can with God's help. Or that chasing after what *you* want doesn't work, but chasing after what *God* wants for you does. Don't let losing discourage you or undermine your worth—learn from it instead.

> *Lord, help me remember that losing is a*
> *chance to learn something new, amen.*

TODAY WITH JESUS . . . LEARN FROM YOUR LOSSES.

THE JUSTICE PART

The Lord loves justice. He will not leave those who worship him.
PSALM 37:28

Y ou're just so angry at that person, you want to forget she exists. So why does she keep popping into your thoughts? God probably brings her to mind because He knows you need to forgive her. And you know you should, so why don't you let go of your anger and forgive? Are you afraid God will be too easy on her? That He won't be fair? That there won't be justice for your hurts?

These kinds of feelings are nothing new. Remember Paul? Before he decided to follow Jesus, he terrorized the Christians. But after Paul became a follower, God challenged those same Christians to forgive Paul. It wasn't easy, but they did—and their forgiveness set Paul free to become one of the greatest preachers of Christ ever (Acts 8–9).

So forgive. Trust God to handle the justice part. Because you never know what God will do through you—or through that person who hurt you.

Dear God, please show me those I need to forgive and help me to do it, amen.

TODAY WITH JESUS . . . LET GO OF REVENGE.

KNOCKING DOWN WALLS

Now, shout! The Lord has given you this city!
JOSHUA 6:16

Joshua looked at the wall that towered all around the city of Jericho. Taking over this city would be a huge task—there just didn't seem to be any way through this wall. But God had promised Israel would win, and Joshua believed Him.

Israel *did* win. For years after, children would ask their parents how the wall had come down. And their parents would answer that it wasn't with battering rams or military strategy. The wall was knocked down by obedience. God said shout, so the people of Israel shouted—and the wall came tumbling down (Joshua 6).

Is there a wall in your life? Not a brick or stone wall, but an obstacle keeping you from where you want to go? Learn from Joshua and the Israelites. Obeying God—not your own plans or strength—is the answer. Talk to God, and do exactly what He says. Then shout His praises as the wall comes tumbling down.

Lord, I give You all the walls—the obstacles—in my life. I know You can knock them down, amen.

**TODAY WITH JESUS . . . PRAISE HIM
FOR LEADING YOU TO VICTORY.**

FACTS, NOT FEELINGS

God's judgment is right, and as a result you will be
counted worthy of the kingdom of God.

2 THESSALONIANS 1:5 NIV

What do you think about yourself? Do you believe you're a beloved and treasured child of God—not perfect, but still perfectly loved Him? Or do you ever wonder if you're really worth His love? If you're good enough for Him or for anybody?

These feelings of doubt are just that—feelings, not facts. They steal your joy and blind you to who you really are: God's child. If you ever wonder what you're worth, turn to the Bible and what God says about you. *That's* the real truth.

God knows everything about everything, and so He knows exactly what you're worth: You're worth sending His Son to die to save you (John 3:16). You worth being adopted into His family (Romans 8:15). And you're worth listening to (Jeremiah 33:3) and loving (1 John 3:1). If you ever start to feel worthless, just ask God to show you the facts. Trust His Words, not your feelings.

Lord Jesus, thank You for making me worthy of Your love, amen.

TODAY WITH JESUS . . . THINK ABOUT
HOW IMPORTANT YOU ARE TO GOD.

OCTOBER

HAVE YOU BEEN WITH JESUS?

The Jewish leaders saw that Peter and John were not afraid to speak. They understood that these men had no special training or education. So they were amazed. Then they realized that Peter and John had been with Jesus.
ACTS 4:13

Do you obey Jesus because it's the "right thing to do," or because you're really excited about following Him? God wants you to obey Him, but not just because you're supposed to. He wants you to serve Him with joy, because you love Him and are so grateful for all He's done. God wants to pour Himself into you and shine out through you.

When Jesus' disciples Peter and John went out to teach about God, people saw their joy and their love for God. Their words and wisdom were so amazing that people knew it must have come from God—and not from these two ordinary men.

When you make spending time with God an important part of your life, you'll shine with His Spirit too. He'll give you His wisdom, strength, and words. And people will know you've "been with Jesus."

Lord, fill me with Your Spirit so that others will
see You shining through me, amen.

TODAY WITH JESUS . . . SPEND TIME ALONE WITH HIM.

"DON'T"

"You must not eat the fruit from the tree which gives the knowledge of good and evil."

GENESIS 2:17

What would happen if you heard your mom say, "Don't touch that hot stove," but you touched it anyway? Or if you heard your teacher say, "Don't copy off anyone else's paper," but you went ahead and did it? There would be trouble, right? So what do you think would happen if you heard God say "don't," but you did it anyway? Trouble.

Just ask Adam. He heard God say *don't* eat the fruit from the tree of knowledge. And God was very clear—there was no way to misunderstand what He said. But Adam ate from it anyway, and there's been trouble ever since.

When God says "don't," it isn't because He's trying to keep you away from something wonderful. Instead, it's because He's trying to protect you from something that would hurt you, His beloved child. God has so many blessings planned for you—don't mess them up by doing something He says not to do.

*Lord, I'm so sorry for all the times I do the things
You say not to do. Please forgive me, amen.*

TODAY WITH JESUS . . . LISTEN TO HIM AND OBEY.

LIAR, LIAR

Did God really say that you must not eat
fruit from any tree in the garden?
GENESIS 3:1

S atan is the master of lying. He does it better than anyone else ever will. He's sneaky and tricky, and he knows all your weak spots.

Just look at how he tricked Eve. When Satan lied to her, he used almost the exact same words as God. God said, "You are free to eat from any tree in the garden; but you must not eat from the tree of the knowledge of good and evil" (Genesis 2:16–17 NIV). Satan only added one little word: "Did God really say that you must *not* eat fruit from any tree in the garden?" Satan's one extra word made Eve start to question God.

Don't let Satan trick you. If you ever hear him whisper something that *sort of* sounds like what God said, or something that makes you question God, run back to the Bible and check it out. Look at what God *really* said—and obey Him, not the master of lies.

Father, help me recognize the Devil's lies
and follow Your truth instead, amen.

TODAY WITH JESUS . . . READ ABOUT THE POWER OF GOD'S WORD IN HEBREWS 4:12.

HE'S ALWAYS THERE

Jesus stood up and commanded the wind and the
waves to stop. He said, "Quiet! Be still!" Then the
wind stopped, and the lake became calm.

MARK 4:39

A boat caught in a storm gets tossed around by the wind and waves. But think about this: underneath the water, there's no storm. Everything is perfectly still and peaceful.

That's a picture of the peace Jesus promises you. In this world, Jesus said you'll have troubles because you follow Him. There'll be times when you feel like a boat tossed around in a terrible storm. But Jesus also said He would never leave those who follow Him. And because He's with you, you can have His peace even in the most terrible circumstances.

How? Because you know His love for you will never end. He will give you His strength when you're too tired to keep going. And He'll comfort you because He understands everything you're going through. Yes, there will be storms in this world, but remember you're with the One who's already overcome this world (John 16:33).

Thank You, Lord Jesus, for always being with
me—especially in the storms, amen.

TODAY WITH JESUS . . . REMEMBER
JESUS IS ALWAYS WITH YOU.

PEACE IN TIMES OF TROUBLE

God's Spirit, who is in you, is greater than the devil, who is in the world.
1 JOHN 4:4

As hard as it is to face troubles and sadness, those difficult times can actually bring you blessings. *How?* Because hard times let you see how God is working in your life—as He comforts you with His love and fills you with His strength and wisdom. In fact, it's often in the hardest of times that you *know* God is right there with you, as He fills you with joy and peace no matter what's happening around you.

Of course, that doesn't mean difficult times aren't still hard or hurtful. But it does mean that you know you aren't alone and that God is helping you.

Everyone has hard times—even the children of God. *But* as a child of God you have a blessing no one else has: God walks with you and gives you His peace—a peace that says He'll take care of everything, even if you don't see how just yet.

Lord, thank You for walking with me in good
times and in hard times, amen.

**TODAY WITH JESUS . . . BELIEVE HE'S
WITH YOU, NO MATTER WHAT.**

YOUR TEACHER

You will see your teacher with your own eyes.

ISAIAH 30:20

Sometimes things happen that make you feel all alone and unimportant. And there will be days when your friends don't want to listen to your troubles, and you think there's no way your parents would understand. Even the everyday stuff of life—like going to school and practice and hanging out with friends—can feel hard to do. Your hopes and dreams and goals suddenly seem completely impossible. You might even wonder, *What's the point of loving God if things are still going to be this bad?*

Dear child, loving God is *always* worth it. He hasn't left you, but He is teaching you to look for Him in the difficult times. And when you seek Him, He'll show Himself to you in amazing ways! When things seem impossible, remember "for God all things are possible" (Matthew 19:26). Look for Him in good times and in bad times—and let Him show you His love, power, and glory.

Father, thank You for working in my life,
especially in the hard times, amen.

**TODAY WITH JESUS . . . LOOK FOR
WHAT HE'S TEACHING YOU.**

SHARE HIS LOVE

You are all children of God through faith in Christ Jesus.
GALATIANS 3:26 NLT

God's love is for every single person. It doesn't matter how old a person is, where she comes from, or the color of his skin. God's love is for everyone. *But . . .* He has chosen to show His love through those who accept Jesus as their Savior, through His children—through you.

You are God's arms, hands, and feet here on earth. Your job is to show His love to others—to the people who are next door and to those on the other side of the world. Care for them just as He would. Don't judge people by how they look, how much money they have, their skin color or language, or even the mistakes they make. Everyone needs Jesus to save them, no matter who they are.

The Bible says, "When we have the opportunity to help anyone, we should do it" (Galatians 6:10). So try to be more like Jesus—share His love with everyone and do good wherever you go (Acts 10:38). And maybe they will become children of God as well.

*Father, help me see others the way You
see them—with love, amen.*

**TODAY WITH JESUS . . . SHARE GOD'S
LOVE WITH EVERYONE YOU MEET.**

SHARE HIS BLESSINGS

*"The Holy Spirit will come to you. Then you will receive power.
You will be my witnesses . . . in every part of the world."*

ACTS 1:8

God is always speaking to you—through His Word, through the words of others, and through the things that happen in your life. He does this so you can get to know Him and His love. But He also speaks to you so you can share His truth with others.

God's blessings are supposed to be shared. In fact, just before Jesus returned to heaven, He told His disciples to share everything He'd told them. "Go and make followers of all people in the world," Jesus said. "Baptize them in the name of the Father and the Son and the Holy Spirit. Teach them to obey everything that I have told you." And then He promised, "You can be sure that I will be with you always. I will continue with you until the end of the world" (Matthew 28:19–20). Those same words are for you, too: share His blessings.

*Lord, help me tell others about all the
blessings You've given me, amen.*

**TODAY WITH JESUS . . . TALK TO
SOMEONE ABOUT JESUS.**

UNDER ATTACK

Give yourselves to God. Stand against the devil,
and the devil will run away from you.
JAMES 4:7

Have you ever felt like you're under attack by the Devil himself? It's as if he's snuck into your life and is messing up everything he possibly can. And then he sits there and whispers questions in your ear, like, "If God is with you, why is everything going wrong?"

Don't listen to that liar! Stand against him. How? By saying, "I trust Jesus. I love Jesus. And I will follow Him always!" The very best way to silence the Devil and his lies is to say—out loud—how much you love and trust God. The Devil just can't stand to hear those words, so he'll go running.

You don't have to live in fear or worry. Your God will protect you and save you from the evil one. So when your mind starts filling up with doubts, recognize that the Devil is attacking. Send him running by praising the name of Jesus!

Father, thank You for loving me, saving me, and
protecting me from the Devil's lies, amen.

TODAY WITH JESUS . . . PRAISE HIM OUT LOUD.

CHANGE YOUR "INGREDIENTS"

Only the Lord gives wisdom. Knowledge and
understanding come from him.

PROVERBS 2:6

Do you ever feel like you're facing the same issue over and over again? The day is different, the people are different, the place is different, but the problem is the same. Maybe it's losing your temper, lying, or gossiping, but you just can't seem to get free from that particular struggle.

It's like a baker who uses salt instead of sugar to bake a cake. He tries different pans and different ovens, but every cake turns out horrible. The fact is his cake will never be good until he changes his ingredients.

That's true for you too. You can try all different kinds of things to fix your problems, but until you change the "ingredients" inside you, you'll keep getting the same terrible result. Ask God what you need to do. Ask Him to change you on the inside—He'll teach you how to handle your struggles in a way that pleases Him and makes life sweet.

Lord, help me stop making the same mistakes.
Show me what I need to change, amen.

TODAY WITH JESUS . . . BE
TRANSFORMED FROM WITHIN.

A SEASON AND A REASON

*The followers went to Jesus and woke him. They
said, "Master! Master! We will drown!"*

*Jesus got up and gave a command to the wind and the waves. The
wind stopped, and the lake became calm. Jesus said to his followers,
"Where is your faith?"*

LUKE 8:24–25

Jesus never pretended that following Him would be easy. He never
said His followers wouldn't have trouble or sadness. And He didn't
shield them from hard times. Jesus still allowed the storms of life
to come.

But Jesus *did* say that troubles wouldn't last forever. And He
promised not only to walk with you through them, but also to use
them for your good. The storms of this life come only for a season,
and they come for a reason. Don't worry that your troubles will never
go away or that they will crush you.

Jesus is with you *always*. So you don't have to worry over troubles
or let sadness pull you down. You can face the storms of this life,
and—with Jesus by your side—you can overcome them.

*Father, thank You for always watching over me
and loving me—that gives me joy, amen.*

**TODAY WITH JESUS . . . REMEMBER
HE IS YOUR STRENGTH.**

IMAGINING THE WORST

*They will call to me, and I will answer them. I will be with
them in trouble. I will rescue them and honor them.*

PSALM 91:15

Do you always imagine the worst? For example, you forget your
homework do you then imagine being embarrassed in front of
the whole class, which leads to flunking the class, losing all your
friends, and being kicked out of school completely? Imagining the
worst can make even small problems seem like enormous disasters.

When your imagination runs wild, it's time to remember who's
really in control: God. Since the beginning of time He's never lost
control—not even for the blink of an eye. And He's watching over you.

God is your protector. That's His "job." Your "job" is to obey Him
and then trust Him to take care of you. No matter what happens, God
has a plan to bless you and reward you with the blessings of heaven.
He'll use everything you experience—even the "bad" stuff—for your
good *if* you trust Him. Stop imagining the worst, and trust Him to
give you His best.

*Father God, I'm so glad You're in control. Whatever
happens, I know You're taking care of me, amen.*

**TODAY WITH JESUS . . . IMAGINE HIS
BEST, NOT YOUR WORST.**

GOD *WILL*

Those people who go to the Lord for help will have every good thing.
PSALM 34:10

Worry is not part of God's plan for you. He doesn't want you wasting a single second wondering things like, *Does anybody really like me? How will I ever get through school?* Or, *What happens if my mom loses her job?*

God will take care of all your needs. Believe that. There's nothing you need that's too big or too hard for God (Philippians 4:19).

So why do you still worry? Maybe it's because, in your head, you know that God will take care of you, but your heart struggles to believe you can completely trust Him. Here's the truth, plain and simple: God is your provider. When you trust and obey Him, He *will* take care of you and give you everything you need for life and a relationship with Him (2 Peter 1:3).

So whatever it is you need today—peace, a friend, encouragement—trust God to give it to you. Then praise Him for it.

> *Lord, thank You for giving me everything I truly need. I trust You to take care of me, amen.*

**TODAY WITH JESUS . . . BELIEVE HE'LL
GIVE YOU WHAT YOU NEED.**

NO LIMITS

"I came to give life—life in all its fullness."

JOHN 10:10

Isn't today's verse an awesome one? Jesus not only gives you eternal life in heaven when you decide to follow Him as Your Savior, but He also gives you a full life here on earth—a life that's rich and overflowing with every good blessing, so that you can do all He created you to do.

That sounds amazing, but what does it look like in real life? It means if you lose a friend, He has a new one waiting for you. It means if you don't make the team, He's got something better planned for you. Just think of all the ways God has taken care of His people: manna from heaven (Exodus 16:35), water from a rock (Exodus 17:6), feeding thousands with one little boy's lunch (Matthew 14:14–21)—and those are just a few examples. God's power is unlimited and awesome. He'll never let you down (Habakkuk 3:17–19).

Lord, thank You for loving me and using Your power to take care of me, amen.

TODAY WITH JESUS . . . THERE'S NO LIMIT TO WHAT HE CAN DO.

OCTOBER 15

ENJOY BEING YOU!

God began by making one man. From him came all the different people who live everywhere in the world. He decided exactly when and where they must live. God wanted them to look for him. . . . "By his power we live and move and exist."
ACTS 17:26–28

Have you ever wished you were more like someone else? That you could sing like her or paint like him or be as popular as they are? Do you wish you had the gifts God gave to others? Or are you happy with who He made you to be and the skills He's given you?

Dear one, *you are special*. God created you and gave you just the right gifts, personality, and talents that you need to live out His uniquely wonderful plan for you. And when you accept Jesus as your Savior, He gives you spiritual gifts, too—like encouragement, teaching, or serving—to use for His glory (Ephesians 2:10).

Rejoice in the fact that you are God's beloved child whom He created in "an amazing and wonderful way" (Psalm 139:14). There's never been—and will never be—anyone else just like you. So enjoy being you!

Father, help me enjoy being the person
You created me to be, amen.

TODAY WITH JESUS . . . DISCOVER
WHO HE CREATED YOU TO BE.

DESIGNED TO NEED GOD

I do not mean that we are able to say that we can do this work
ourselves. It is God who makes us able to do all that we do.
2 CORINTHIANS 3:5

Do you ever feel like you just can't do the things you're supposed to do today? Or do you ever worry you'll completely mess up and fall on your face?

That's actually not a bad thing. Why? Because admitting that you can't do it all by yourself is also admitting that you need God—and that's a wonderful thing. In fact, that's the way He designed you. You see, God has filled you up with abilities and gifts and talents, and you can do some pretty good things with them on your own. But you can do *amazing* and *extraordinary* things with them when you depend on Him to help you. And those things are what let other people see Him working through you.

So today, don't say, "I can't." Instead, trust God and declare for all the world to see, "With God's help, I can!"

Lord Jesus, I will trust You to help me do
whatever You want me to do, amen.

TODAY WITH JESUS . . . ADMIT YOU NEED HIS HELP.

OCTOBER 17

JESUS SAVES

Anyone who asks the Lord for help will be saved.
ACTS 2:21

Some people believe, "I've sinned too much to be saved," "God will never forgive me for that," or even "I messed up, and I don't think I'm saved anymore."

If these are things you've ever worried or wondered about, remember this: Jesus took care of all these things on the cross. First, when you decide to follow Him and accept Him as your Savior, every one of your sins is forgiven. *Every single one.* And second, when you love Jesus, there's no sin too big for Him to forgive. And finally, nothing you do will change God's love for you. Your salvation is a free gift from Jesus—you can't earn it by being perfect and you can't lose it by messing up.

Don't worry—Jesus *will* save you. Trust His love, obey His commands, and believe He's taken care of your sins on the cross. Then live your life as a "thank You" to Him.

Father, thank You for saving me. I want to live
a life that praises You always, amen.

TODAY WITH JESUS . . . REST IN KNOWING
YOU'RE SAFE WITH JESUS.

DISAPPOINTMENTS

Should we take only good things from God and not trouble?

JOB 2:10

Wow! That was *not* how you expected things to go—what a disappointment! Now you have a choice to make: Will you blame God for letting you down? Or will you trust Him to do something good with this disappointment?

Remember Job? He lost everything—his riches, his children, and even his health. Then Job's wife tried to get him to blame God for all his troubles. But Job wouldn't listen. He chose to trust God. And because he did, God blessed Job with more riches, more children, and good health (Job 42:10–17).

The way you choose to handle disappointment is so important. Don't listen when the Devil says, "Blame God," "You're not worthy," or, "God doesn't love you anymore." Trust that God has a perfect plan for everything in your life—even this disappointment. If something doesn't work out, it's because God has something much better waiting for you.

Father, this isn't what I wanted, but I trust that
it's part of Your best plan for me, amen.

**TODAY WITH JESUS . . . LOOK FOR THE
GOOD AFTER A DISAPPOINTMENT.**

GETTING RID OF GUILT

Lord, I give my life to you. Lord, you are kind and forgiving.
You have great love for those who call to you.
PSALM 86:4–5

*R*egret is just a fancy word for guilt. It's what you feel when you have the chance to do something good—but you don't. Perhaps you didn't treat that person with love, or you didn't help when you could have, or you made a bad choice because you didn't talk to God first. You blew it, and now you're paying for it with these horrible feelings of guilt.

Dear child, if that happens to you, don't keep living with regret. Go to God, ask Him to forgive you, and let go of the guilt. God may ask you to fix your mistake, to make it right with those you've hurt, or to forgive anyone who's hurt you. If He does, obey Him immediately. But then move on. Don't keep beating yourself up over something that God has already forgiven. Forgive yourself too.

Father God, thank You for forgiving me. Please
help me to forgive myself, amen.

TODAY WITH JESUS . . . LET HIM TAKE AWAY YOUR GUILT.

GOD'S MESSENGER

The Lord spoke to Paul in a vision and told him,
"Don't be afraid! Speak out! Don't be silent!"

ACTS 18:9 NLT

Ancient Corinth was a tough place to live, especially if you were a Christian. Located by the sea, its busy port brought visitors from all over the world. But those visitors brought with them idol worship, wicked ways, and sinfulness of every kind.

Corinth desperately needed to hear the good news of Jesus. And with all those visitors, a lot of people could be reached. So God sent Paul to Corinth. And even though a lot of the people wanted him to be quiet, Paul still told them about Jesus.

God may also ask you to go somewhere where people don't want to hear about Jesus—and it just might be in your own school or neighborhood! But don't be afraid and don't be silent. God knows everything you're facing, and He'll give you the courage and the words to speak. You're His messenger for Jesus—and the world needs to hear what He wants you to say.

Lord, give me the courage to tell others about Jesus, amen.

TODAY WITH JESUS . . . TELL SOMEONE
THE GOOD NEWS TODAY.

NEVER ALONE

"I loved you as the Father loved me. Now remain in my love."
JOHN 15:9

When you're feeling left out or lonely, there's a way to feel better instantly—*stop* thinking about what you don't have and *start* thinking about what you do have. And what do you have? God!

Once you decide to follow Jesus and accept Him as your Savior, you're never alone again. His Holy Spirit actually comes to live inside you.

The Spirit of God not only lives in you, but He also wants you to live in Him. That means talking to Him about everything, reading and thinking about His Word, trusting Him to take care of you, and obeying Him in every part of your life. It takes practice—and you won't be perfect at it. But as you try to live in Him, God will pull you closer and closer to Himself. He'll show you that He's always with you and always working in your life. And you never have to be lonely again.

Jesus, thank You for Your wonderful presence that is always with me. I know I'm never alone, amen.

TODAY WITH JESUS . . . ENJOY BEING WITH HIM.

"POOR"

"Accept my teachings and learn from me, because I am gentle and humble in spirit, and you will find rest for your lives."

MATTHEW 11:29 NCV

Think about this: everyone you meet today is "poor" in some way. They may be impoverished from a lack of money or possessions. But they might also be "poor" from a broken heart, a past mistake, or a dream that didn't come true. That's called being "poor in spirit," and it can be just as hard as being deprived of things.

Whether your trouble and sadness are because of something that happened to you or because of something you did, they still hurt. And unless you deal with your feelings, you'll just keep on hurting. So how can you work through your emotions? Well, the fact is that you can't—at least, not on your own. You need Jesus' help, and He's so ready to give it. He says, "Blessed are the poor in spirit, for theirs is the kingdom of heaven" (Matthew 5:3 NASB).

So ask Jesus. Tell Him about whatever is hurting you and trust Him to take care of it. He'll carry your burdens for you, and give you rest and peace.

Jesus, I am poor in many ways. Please fill me with the riches of Your presence, amen.

TODAY WITH JESUS . . . LET HIM BLESS YOU WITH HIS RICHES.

LISTEN TO THE HOLY SPIRIT

"The Helper will teach you everything. He will cause you to remember all the things I told you."
JOHN 14:26

God still speaks today—through Scripture, through the words of others, or through the things that happen in your life. But it's the Holy Spirit that helps you listen and hear what God is saying to you.

You see, when you follow Jesus, the Holy Spirit comes to live inside you. Then, when you pray, it isn't God up in heaven listening to you way down here on earth—with thousands of miles separating you. Instead, the Holy Spirit of God is *right there inside you*, helping you pray and helping you hear God's response.

But how can you know what the Spirit is telling you? By listening and believing He's able to answer you and guide you. Just as you trust Jesus to save you, you must also trust the Holy Spirit to lead you. So today, humbly bow before God in prayer—and count on the Holy Spirit to tell you God's answer.

Lord, thank You for Your Holy Spirit, who lives in me and helps me hear what You have to say, amen.

TODAY WITH JESUS . . . LISTEN WHEN YOU PRAY.

YOUR TIME WITH HIM

"Always remember what is written in the Book of the Teachings. Study it day and night. Then you will be sure to obey everything that is written there."

JOSHUA 1:8

*M*editation is simply taking time to think about something. When you are a follower of Jesus, meditation—thinking about Him, His power, and His Word—is so very important.

Many people think they're much too busy to "just sit and think" about God. But when you take time to be with God, He actually helps you get through your busiest times. He clears away the confusing "stuff" and helps you see what you truly need to do. Time with Him also helps you get to know Him better, so that it's easier to recognize His voice above all the "noise" of this world.

God doesn't just want grown-ups to meditate on Him each day—He wants you to meditate too. And it isn't hard. Begin by sitting alone, reading a passage of the Bible, and being quiet with God. Think about Him—about what He is teaching you in His Word. Listen to His voice, be filled with His peace, and let His Spirit guide you.

Lord, help me understand that I'm never too busy for You. Fill my thoughts with the wonder of You, amen.

TODAY WITH JESUS . . . MEDITATE ON HIM.

EVERYTHING YOU NEED

"Come to me, all of you who are tired and have heavy loads. I will give you rest."
MATTHEW 11:28

Some days are just rough. Everything seems to go wrong. And by the end of the day, you're worn out and feeling completely defeated. During times like that, remember this: the tougher your day is, the more you need to spend time with God. When everything is going wrong, sitting still with God may seem like the last thing you have time for—but it's the one thing that will help you the most.

Take a moment and tell God everything that's happening. Admit how you're really feeling—it's okay, He already knows you're feeling helpless and maybe even scared. Tell Him your sins and the things you wish you'd done differently. Tell Him your worries and fears. Ask for His forgiveness, His strength, and His peace. And then listen as His Spirit speaks love and encouragement straight to your heart.

When this world wears you out, go to Him—and He'll bless you with everything you need.

Lord, some days are just rough. Thank You for being a place where I can find rest and the strength to keep going, amen.

TODAY WITH JESUS . . . LET HIM GIVE YOU WHAT YOU NEED.

LIGHT CHASES AWAY DARKNESS

*"I am the light of the world. The person who follows me will
never live in darkness. He will have the light that gives life."*

JOHN 8:12

Walking into a dark room can be frightening. Why? Because you don't know what's in there or what's going to happen. In the same way, there can be dark places in your life that frighten you—because you don't know what's really going on in those parts of your life. But don't be afraid. God wants to shine His light into those dark places.

Remember, in the beginning, God spoke and light was created—and He did that before He created the sun, moon, and stars (Genesis 1). That's because the very presence of God gives light (Revelation 22:5). It's not just light you can see with your eyes, but a spiritual light you can feel with your heart.

So when the darkness of fear or worry starts creeping up on you, run to Him. Stand with the Father in His light, and you'll have nothing to fear.

*Lord, light up my life with Your presence and
chase away all my worries and fears, amen.*

TODAY WITH JESUS . . . SOAK IN HIS LIGHT.

NO BETTER ROAD MAP

Lord, teach me your ways. Guide me to do what is right.
PSALM 27:11

When you're lost and don't know how to get where you're going, do you like to admit it? Most people don't. In fact, most people will spend hours trying to find their own way, rather than stop and ask for help.

That can happen as Christians too. For example, you may *know* God has a perfect path planned for your life, but do you ask Him to show you the way? Or do you try to figure it out for yourself? Because the thing is, God's path isn't something you'll just accidentally stumble onto or find on your own. Only He can show you which way to go—step by step—as you spend time with Him.

If you want to know God's path for you, just stop and ask Him for directions. He knows exactly where you are, where you need to go, and how to get you there.

> *Father, forgive me for wandering around on my own. Please show me the way to go, amen.*

TODAY WITH JESUS . . . ASK HIM WHICH WAY TO GO.

TRANSFORMED

Offer your lives as a living sacrifice to him. Your offering must be only for God and pleasing to him. This is the spiritual way for you to worship. Do not be shaped by this world. Instead be changed within by a new way of thinking.

ROMANS 12:1–2

Today's verse gives you three goals for your life as a Christian. The first is to offer your life as a living sacrifice to God. That means to live in a way that obeys and pleases Him—even when it's not what you want to do, like being kind to your enemies.

The second goal is to not be shaped by this world. That means doing what God says is right, even when all your friends are telling you it's okay to do what He says is wrong. And the third goal is to be changed inside by a new way of thinking. That means letting God's love and kindness replace your own selfish thoughts.

These three things will transform you and make you more and more like Jesus—like the person God created you to be. It won't be easy, and you'll need His help every day. But it will be so worth it!

Lord, I offer You my whole life. Make me into the person You created me to be, amen.

TODAY WITH JESUS . . . LET HIM CHANGE YOU.

EVERY NEED OF YOUR HEART

It is better to trust the Lord than to trust people.
PSALM 118:8

You may think, *If only she'd be my friend, my life would be complete,* or *If only he'd pick me for his team, life would be awesome,* or *If only my parents wouldn't get a divorce, I'd be happy.*

But the truth is being popular, making the team, or even having everything perfect at home won't make your life complete. Only God knows what your heart really needs. Only He can supply the empty places of your heart. And only He will never, ever let you down.

But remember, your God is also a jealous God. He wants to be first in your life. And a beautiful thing happens when you put God first—every other relationship and friendship in your life gets even better. So put Him first in your time and in your thoughts, and trust Him to meet every need of your heart.

Father, please help me put You first in my life,
and forgive me when I don't, amen.

TODAY WITH JESUS . . . PUT HIM FIRST.

WHAT GOD IS REALLY LIKE

"The Son of Man came to find lost people and save them."

LUKE 19:10

What is God really like? That's actually an easy question to answer. You can see God—and what He's really like—in the life of Jesus.

Jesus treated everyone with kindness and respect. He was always loving and giving, even to people like Zacchaeus. Zacchaeus was a tax collector for Rome. He was hated by everyone because he cheated the people by taking too much money. But when Jesus came to town, He didn't ignore or scold him. Instead, Jesus told Zacchaeus to climb down from that sycamore tree he was in so that he could be saved.

All through the books of Matthew, Mark, Luke, and John, you see Jesus healing, comforting, and helping people. He wept when His friends hurt, laughed when they were happy, and forgave them of their sins.

That's who God really is—holy, kind, powerful, and loving. Read His Word, get to know Him, and see for yourself what He's really like.

Lord, show me through Your Word who You really are, amen.

TODAY WITH JESUS . . . READ ABOUT ZACCHAEUS IN LUKE 19:1–10.

THE ARMS OF GOD

*God, your love is so precious! You protect people as
a bird protects her young under her wings.*
PSALM 36:7

You know God is with you . . . but have you ever wondered what it
would feel like to be wrapped up in His arms, completely safe and
secure? You can know that too.

One way is through the people God sends to help you and hold
you. Your friends and those who love and care for you are Jesus'
physical arms on this earth. But another way is through the peace
and comfort He gives you Himself. There will be times—when you're
with Him in His presence—that you can almost physically feel Him
reach down and cradle you in His arms. And your heart will be filled
with a perfect peace as He holds you close.

If you need to feel God near you today, sit with Him quietly. Wait
for Him, until you feel His loving presence with you—He will come
and wrap you in His arms.

*Father God, I need You today. Hold me
in Your loving arms, amen.*

TODAY WITH JESUS . . . LET HIM HOLD YOU.

NOVEMBER

DO YOU NEED TO FORGIVE?

If we confess our sins, he will forgive our sins. We can trust God. He does what is right. He will make us clean from all the wrongs we have done.
1 JOHN 1:9

Forgiving can be a very hard thing to do. But *not* forgiving can cause all sorts of problems in your life and in your relationship with God. Take a look at your heart—is there anyone you need to forgive?

You may think you're not holding a grudge, but ask yourself these questions: Do you secretly hope someone will get what he or she deserves? Is there someone you talk badly about? Do you daydream about getting even with someone? Do you keep thinking about what that person did to you? Do you feel happy when something bad happens to someone who hurt your feelings?

If you answered yes to any of these questions, you have some forgiving to do. Ask God to search your heart and show you who you need to forgive. Then ask Him to forgive you—and to help you forgive the one who hurt you.

Lord, help me forgive others completely—
the same way You forgive me, amen.

TODAY WITH JESUS . . . IS THERE SOMEONE YOU NEED TO FORGIVE?

GOD HAS PLANS FOR YOU

"I know what I have planned for you. . . . I plan
to give you hope and a good future."

JEREMIAH 29:11

God knows exactly where you are and what you're doing right this very second. No matter what the world says, you're not just some accident of evolution, bouncing along through time and space.

The God who created this universe and carefully placed each star in the sky also created you. And He has carefully planned a bright and shining future for you. And that bright future isn't just in heaven—it starts here on earth. God has great plans for you!

As a child of God, your future in heaven is secure. But God is also interested in the details of your life today. All the joys and troubles that you want to tell your best friend? God wants you to tell Him, too. Make Him part of your everyday life. Not only does He want to know, but He also has things to show you and places for you to go.

Father, even though You created absolutely everything, You
still want to spend time with me. You are amazing, amen.

TODAY WITH JESUS . . . TELL GOD ABOUT YOUR DAY.

OKAY TO BE ANGRY?

You forgive us. So you are respected.
PSALM 130:4

Some people say it's okay for them to be angry when someone has wronged them. They even have a fancy name for it: "righteous indignation." And they'll talk about how Jesus turned over the money changers' tables and blasted the religious leaders.

The thing is, Jesus was angry because the money changers were misrepresenting God and hurting others' relationships with the Lord by doing so. So Jesus' anger motivated Him to make things right—to teach people how to follow God the right way.

That's the big difference. If your anger doesn't motivate you to help people get right with God—if you just wants to get even—that's not okay. *Even if you were wronged.*

If someone has sinned against you, Jesus expects you to forgive—just as He forgave those who put Him on the cross. Don't use fancy words like "righteous indignation" to try to make your anger okay. That doesn't please God. Instead, forgive and let go of that anger.

> *Lord, is there someone I need to forgive? Please show me so that I can make things right with them and You, amen.*

TODAY WITH JESUS . . . FORGIVE THOSE WHO WRONG YOU.

GIVE MERCY ANYWAY

The payment for sin is death. But God gives us the
free gift of life forever in Christ Jesus our Lord.

ROMANS 6:23

Has someone hurt you this week? Was it on purpose? And if it was, what do you think you should you do now?

The natural thing is to want to get even. After all, you deserve to be treated with love, kindness, and respect. Right? Yes, but . . . what about all the times you didn't offer love, kindness, and respect to those around you? How easy it is to forget about all the times you've wronged God by not loving others and not obeying Him.

God's Word says, "Forgive each other just as God forgave you in Christ" (Ephesians 4:32). Remember all that Jesus suffered so that you could be forgiven. No one deserves His grace and mercy, but He gave it anyway. Even if that person you're angry with doesn't deserve your love and compassion, give it anyway—because you're so thankful for all that Jesus has given you.

Lord, thank You for forgiving me. Teach me
to forgive the way You do, amen.

TODAY WITH JESUS . . . GIVE AS
JESUS HAS GIVEN TO YOU.

IN CONTROL

Jesus said to Peter, "Put your sword back. Shall I not drink of the cup the Father has given me?"
JOHN 18:11

You might as well admit it: the reason you get so upset sometimes is because you can't control what's happening in your life. Your plans just aren't working out, and you *don't* like it!

The apostle Peter struggled with the same thing. One minute he's pulling out his sword and ready to fight for Jesus (John 18:10–11), but the next minute he's so afraid that he pretends he doesn't even know Jesus (vv. 25–27)! Perhaps it was because his plans had fallen apart, and he had no control over what was happening. Peter understood how to fight with swords, but he didn't understand how Jesus' death on the cross would lead to an even greater victory—the victory over sin.

Peter wanted to serve God, but he didn't understand God's plan. The same thing will happen to you. God works in mysterious ways—so He won't always act in ways you understand. But trust that He's in control and follow Him anyway—because He's always triumphant!

*Jesus, I don't always understand Your ways, but
I know they're better than mine, amen.*

TODAY WITH JESUS . . . BE GLAD HE'S IN CONTROL.

ALWAYS WILLING

Jesus touched the man and said, "I want to heal you. Be healed!"
MATTHEW 8:3

The poor man kneeling at Jesus' feet was cursed with leprosy. This disease was so terrible that lepers were forced to wear bells so that others could hear them coming and avoid even touching them. It was a lonely, painful, and embarrassing disease.

When Jesus passed by, one brave leper said, "Lord, you have the power to heal me if you want" (Matthew 8:2). The leper knew Jesus *could* heal him, but would He *be willing* to do so? In fact, Jesus *was* willing. He healed the man, *and* He touched him—something no one had done in a very long time.

Hear this truth: Jesus is always willing to heal whatever hurts you. Sometimes He'll mend your body or take away your trouble. And sometimes He'll give you strength and comfort your heart so that you have peace even in the middle of your troubles. But He is always willing to help—just ask.

*Lord, I bow down at Your feet. Please
heal the hurts in my life, amen.*

TODAY WITH JESUS . . . LET HIM HEAL YOUR HURTS.

THE PRICE IS PAID

You were bought by God for a price. So honor God with your bodies.
1 CORINTHIANS 6:20

Busted. You didn't finish your homework, but you're sneaking in some screen time anyway—then your mom walks in. What will she do? What price will you have to pay?

Getting caught by your mom seems very real. But do you ever wonder about getting caught by God? You're doing something you know you shouldn't—watching that show with all the bad language, gossiping, lying, letting your anger get out of control. If God suddenly walked into the room and caught you, what would you do?

The truth is, God is already in the room. He sees everything you do. And there's a price to pay for your sins. But here's the amazing news: Jesus already paid the price for you! You don't have to be punished for your sins. Of course, that doesn't mean you get to go out and do whatever you want. Instead, show how thankful you are by obeying Him.

*Jesus, thank You for paying the price for my sins. Help me
live in a way that helps others learn about You, amen.*

TODAY WITH JESUS . . . HONOR HIM WITH ALL YOU DO.

FACING MOUNTAINS

"If your faith is as big as a mustard seed, you can say to this mountain, 'Move from here to there.' And the mountain will move. All things will be possible for you."

MATTHEW 17:20

Being a child of God means you're promised a lot of wonderful things—a home in heaven, God always by your side, peace, and forgiveness of your sins. But it doesn't mean you're promised an easy life. There will be mountains to climb—like problems, sadness, and hard times. When you face one of those mountains, what will you do? Give up?

No!

When God allows a mountain to come into your life, put your trust in Him—He'll either move that mountain or make sure you have everything you need to climb over it. But you must trust Him to help you—no matter how big that mountain of trouble is. Hold tight to God, and let Him guide you. He will make a way for you, and He won't let you fall.

Lord, sometimes the mountains seem so big, but I know You are bigger. Thank You for making a way for me, amen.

TODAY WITH JESUS . . . REMEMBER GOD IS BIGGER THAN ANY TROUBLE.

SET YOURSELF FREE

"If your brother sins against you seven times in one day, but he says that he is sorry each time, then forgive him."
LUKE 17:4

Is there someone you haven't forgiven? When people hurt you, it's easy for anger and bitterness to creep into your heart. And if you aren't careful, they'll stay there. Too many times, people ignore what the Bible says about forgiving, and they decide to stay angry and get even instead.

But when you're filled with bitterness, you're setting yourself up for an attack by the Devil. He likes to tell you lies like, "You were hurt, so it's okay to be upset. Keep thinking about getting even—he deserves it." And as long as you let Satan keep whispering those lies, you'll stay stuck in your anger and bitterness.

That's not what Jesus wants for you, and that's why He commands you to forgive. Your anger doesn't hurt the one who wronged you. It only hurts you. So if you're holding a grudge, let it go. Forgive that person—and set yourself free.

Lord, if there is anyone I need to forgive,
please show me, amen.

TODAY WITH JESUS . . . LET GO OF ANY ANGER.

IMPOSSIBLE POSSIBLE

God will let Gideon defeat Midian and the whole army!
JUDGES 7:14

Gideon knew all about fear and feeling hopeless. God called him—and a *very* small army—to defeat the massive and mighty army of the Midianites. *Impossible!* There was no way that would work. Then God gave Gideon the news: his very small army was about to be made *even* smaller. Why? So that when Gideon and his army won, everyone would know that it was really God who had fought for them.

Have you ever had to do something you thought was impossible—and then suddenly it got even harder? When that happens, your only choice is to trust God to get you through. And the fact is, the more impossible your challenge seems, the more power God will give you and the more glory He will receive when everything works out.

If your situation looks impossible, trust God. His power makes the impossible possible.

Lord, You are so powerful that You can make impossible things possible. Thank You for Your strength, amen.

**TODAY WITH JESUS . . . LET GOD TURN
THE IMPOSSIBLE INTO POSSIBLE.**

FREEZE

"The message is crowded out by the worries of this life, the lure of wealth, and the desire for other things, so no fruit is produced."
MARK 4:18–19 NLT

Have you ever played freeze tag? Once you're tagged, you can't move—almost like you're paralyzed—until someone else sets you free. Freeze tag is a fun game to play with friends. But there's something else that can make you freeze up that isn't so fun: fear.

Fear—and its close friend, worry—can paralyze you and keep you from doing the things you need and want to do. And often, your fear isn't about something that's really happening. Instead, you're scared of what *might* happen or of not knowing what will happen. Just like the game, fear makes you freeze up and keeps you from moving. But also just like the game, there's a way to be set free: trust God. He knows everything that's going to happen today, tomorrow, and for all eternity. And when you trust Him, He'll make sure you're ready for whatever comes—so you don't have to fear.

Lord, I don't know what my future holds, but You do. I trust You to get me through it, amen.

TODAY WITH JESUS . . . YOU ARE SAFE.

GOD'S WORD

"The thing you should seek is God's kingdom. Then all the other things you need will be given to you."

LUKE 12:31

Once you become a Christian, what does God expect of you? How does He want you to live and treat others?

The answers to these questions—and many more—are found in God's Word. And a great place to start reading is in the Gospels, especially the book of John. Enjoy being with Jesus by reading His Word, talking to Him, and listening to Him. Get to know the kind of person He was and the kind of God He is. Try to understand His words, why He came, and how much He loves you.

And then start reading the Psalms. There you'll find that David went through just about every kind of trouble you can imagine. He asked lots of questions, and he got angry, sad, and mad. In the Psalms, you'll see that you're not alone in your questions, worries, and troubles—and you'll see that God is always there to help you through.

Jesus, show me who You are through Your Word. I want to know You, amen.

TODAY WITH JESUS . . . GET TO KNOW HIM.

BE THE BEST YOU

*The woman . . . said to the people, "A man told me everything
I have ever done. Come see him. Maybe he is the Christ!"*
JOHN 4:28–29

Do you ever find yourself feeling like you're better than someone else? Do you ever say things like, "At least I don't sin like he does," or "I mess up, but I'm doing better than her"? The thing is, God doesn't judge you based on what other people do.

Remember the woman at the well? She'd been married five times, and when Jesus met her, she was living with a man who wasn't her husband. But Jesus didn't say, "You're a sinner. Don't even talk to Me." Instead, Jesus offered her the living water of His love and mercy (John 4:4–41). And that woman—whose life was so full of sin—went on to bring many people to Jesus.

Every single person can be used by God. So don't judge others or think you're better than them. Instead, obey God and be the best you that you can be—let Him do the rest.

*Jesus, help me to please You by becoming
everything You created me to be, amen.*

**TODAY WITH JESUS . . . REMEMBER,
GOD CAN USE EVERYONE.**

PUT BACK TOGETHER AGAIN

I will give them . . . gladness to replace their sorrow . . .
praise to replace their spirit of sadness.

ISAIAH 61:3

Do you remember the nursery rhyme about Humpty Dumpty? He'd been hurt so badly that all the king's horses and all the king's men couldn't put him back together again.

Some hurts are hard to get over. And some people just keep reliving the same hurt over and over again until it poisons their whole life. Other people try to pretend they were never hurt at all, but that only causes more stress and pain. There's only one way to be completely healed from the things that hurt you: give them to God.

It takes courage to take your hurts to God, especially if you're used to carrying them around. But trust God. Tell Him everything. Then let Him gently heal you with His love and put you back together again. He'll teach you to live life at its very best—with Him.

Father, please heal me from any hurts and help me
be the whole person You created me to be, amen.

TODAY WITH JESUS . . . GIVE HIM YOUR HURTS.

JESUS IS YOUR FRIEND

The Lord . . . was pleased to make you his own people.
1 SAMUEL 12:22

There will be days when you feel alone, misunderstood, left out, and unwanted. On those days, remember Jesus and how very much He loves you.

How can you be sure He loves you? Because that's what Jesus does—and what He's always done since the beginning of creation. In the Old Testament God was constantly reaching out to His people and rescuing them. He wanted to be with them. In the New Testament Jesus knew what it was to be lonely, but He also knew what it was like to be comforted by His Father when even His best friends left Him (John 16:32).

Dear child, Jesus wants you to know that He is always right there with you—closer than the air you breathe. You may *feel* lonely sometimes, but you are never really alone. Jesus is the one friend you'll always have, because He's "the same yesterday, today, and forever" (Hebrews 13:8).

> *Lord Jesus, thank You for always being with me. I know I'm never alone, amen.*

TODAY WITH JESUS . . . BELIEVE THAT HE IS WITH YOU.

STUCK ON REPEAT

Jesus said, "So I also don't judge you. You
may go now, but don't sin again."
JOHN 8:11

The woman must have been completely terrified. She had been caught doing something she knew was wrong, and the law said she should be stoned to death. But did Jesus say, "Yes, stone her"? No! Jesus didn't judge her. He told her to go and leave her past behind her.

But that's not always easy to do.

That's because your mind will often replay your past mistakes—like a playlist stuck on repeat. Or maybe you keep remembering the way others judged you when you messed up. Then guilt starts to drag you down. There's only one way to get rid of that kind of thinking: let Jesus teach you who you really are.

You are not your sins. You are not your mistakes. And you are not what other people think of you. You are a dearly loved child of God, whose sins have been forgiven. So go to Him, and leave your past behind.

Thank You, God, for taking away all my sins. Help me
remember who I really am—Your child, amen.

TODAY WITH JESUS . . . REMEMBER YOU ARE HIS.

HE'LL COME THROUGH

My God will use his wonderful riches in Christ
Jesus to give you everything you need.
PHILIPPIANS 4:19

God is all-powerful, and He knows absolutely everything. He's your heavenly Father who loves you so much that He sent His Son to save you. Since God was willing to give up His own Son, shouldn't you trust Him to give you everything you need each day?

God *will* give you what you need—that's His responsibility. Your responsibility is to trust Him, obey Him, and put Him first in your life. Think about Him and all that He blesses you with.

Sadly, it's much easier to think about what you *don't* have—and then you can be tempted to start figuring out a way to get it for yourself. The thing is, the stuff you try to get for yourself is never as good as the blessings God has planned for you. Trust Him to give you everything you need. He'll always come through for you.

> *Father, You always keep Your promises. I'll trust*
> *You to take care of everything I need, amen.*

TODAY WITH JESUS . . . PRAISE HIM
FOR TAKING CARE OF YOU.

SAFE AND SECURE

"I am the Lord. I do not change. So you . . . have not been destroyed."

MALACHI 3:6

Do you trust God to take care of you and to keep you safe and secure? Do you keep your thoughts on Him and not on all the terrible stories you hear on the news? Because if you take your thoughts off God and focus on what's happening in the world, you'll find plenty of things to worry about. This world is a mess! And it's changing all the time.

But God never changes, and He knows absolutely everything, He's more powerful than anything in this world, and He's always with you. He knows what frightens you and what you have to face. He is the Lord of all creation, and He is in control.

You can't count on this world, but you can count on God—to guide you and help you in all things. So no matter what happens, trust Him. God will keep you safe and secure.

Lord, I'm so thankful that You're in control. I trust You to keep me safe and secure, amen.

**TODAY WITH JESUS . . . THANK HIM
FOR WATCHING OVER YOU.**

WHEN FRIENDS DISAPPEAR

The first time I defended myself, no one helped me. Everyone left me. . . . But the Lord stayed with me. He gave me strength.
2 TIMOTHY 4:16–17

When you're having a bad day or a big problem, does it ever seem like all your friends disappear just when you need them most? Why is that? One reason may be that they don't realize how much you need them and how much their presence helps you. But remember this: even when it seems like everyone has deserted you, you are never really alone.

The apostle Paul was facing his last court trial, and he was facing it all by himself because his friends had all left him. But he wasn't really alone. God was with him, and He blessed Paul with courage and strength during that terrible time (2 Timothy 4).

The same will be true for you. When you feel left out, deserted, and alone, God will be with you. Look for Him, and He will bless you with all the strength, comfort, and friendship you need to make it through.

Father, I know You'll never desert me or leave
me all alone. Thank You, amen.

TODAY WITH JESUS . . . YOU ARE NEVER ALONE.

CHOOSE GOD

We have no power against this large army that is attacking us.
We don't know what to do. So we look to you for help.

2 CHRONICLES 20:12

King Jehoshaphat had a choice to make. The enormous armies of the Moabites, Ammonites, and Meunites had joined together for one reason: to destroy Jehoshaphat and the people of God. But instead of preparing his army or trying to figure out how to defeat his enemies, King Jehoshaphat made a different choice. He chose to lead the people in a prayer telling God they were counting on Him to save them. Jehoshaphat was wise enough to know that his nation couldn't survive without God's help—so he did exactly what the Father asked.

When you're faced with a situation where defeat seems almost certain, remember Jehoshaphat's choice. Don't run away in fear. And don't let the Devil lie to you and make you think there is no hope. Turn to the Lord in prayer. Bow down before Him. Admit that you can't handle this on your own and you need His help. Then trust God to do the impossible and lead you to victory.

Father, thank You for being a God I can
turn to when I need help, amen.

TODAY WITH JESUS . . . TRUST GOD, NO MATTER WHAT.

BECAUSE HE GIVES

Every good action and every perfect gift is from God.
JAMES 1:17

Today, thank God for what you have. You may not have everything you want, and you may think you don't have enough. But thank God anyway. Why? Because He is the Lord, and without His goodness, you wouldn't have anything at all. So it's important to admit He's the One who gives you every good thing you have.

But also remember: "Trust in your money and down you go! But the godly flourish like leaves in spring" (Proverbs 11:28 NLT). That means, it doesn't matter *how much* you have. What matters is *how you use* what you have. Are you selfish, or are you willing to share? Do you take credit for what you have, or do you thank God?

"Those who trust in the LORD will lack no good thing" (Psalm 34:10 NLT). Trust Him to give you what you need and then praise Him!

> *Lord, thank You for all You've given me. I know*
> *You'll give me everything I really need, amen.*

**TODAY WITH JESUS . . . THANK HIM
FOR ALL HE'S GIVEN YOU.**

WORSHIP HIM

Praise the Lord our God. Worship at the Temple, his footstool.

PSALM 99:5

You were created to worship God. So why is it sometimes so hard to bow down at His feet and truly adore Him? Why is it easier to tell Him about everything that's wrong in your life than it is to tell Him how awesome He is?

One reason might be your pride. You're too busy thinking about yourself instead of your amazing Savior. Another reason might be sin—you've tried to get what you want your own way, instead of trusting God to give you what you need.

It's only when you bow down at His feet and truly worship the Lord that He blesses you with His peace and freedom. Focus on God and His holy majesty, unlimited power, wisdom, and unending love for you. Worship Him—and enjoy simply being with the One who loves you most of all.

Lord, You are Lord of all creation. I praise You and worship
You for who You are and all You've done, amen.

TODAY WITH JESUS . . . BOW DOWN AND WORSHIP HIM.

A SPIRIT OF PRAISE

"True worshipers will worship the Father in spirit and truth."
JOHN 4:23

When you're in church, do you feel God with you? When you're having your own quiet time alone with Him, can you tell that He's there? Maybe you see other people praising God, but you don't feel what they seem to be feeling. And you wonder if you're really reaching God.

Know this: in the same way that you can know facts about God without really knowing Him personally, you can say the words "I love You, Lord," and "I thank You, Lord" without really praising Him.

Real praise comes when you give yourself completely to God. Paul says, "Be filled with the Spirit"—that's the Holy Spirit of God (Ephesians 5:18). *Then* you can "sing and make music in your hearts to the Lord" (v. 19). You can only truly praise God when you let His Spirit fill you. And you do that by giving God control of your life.

> *Lord, show me how to really praise You—*
> *with my words and my life, amen.*

**TODAY WITH JESUS . . . PRAISE HIM
WITH YOUR WHOLE HEART.**

LOOK. SEARCH. AND FIND.

"Those people honor me who give me offerings to show thanks. And I, God, will save those who do that."

PSALM 50:23

Today, give God a sacrifice of thanksgiving. That simply means give Him your time, your thoughts, and your praise because you're so thankful for all He's done for you. Even if everything seems to be going wrong, praise Him anyway. How do you do that?

Look. Search. And *find* reasons to be grateful. Even on your absolute worst day there are blessings all around you. Remember all the ways He's helped you in the past. Praise Him for who He is, how much He loves you, and for saving you. Make a list of every blessing Jesus gives you—like forgiveness, peace, and joy. Think about God's promises—like how He will love you always and will never leave you. Ask the Holy Spirit to open your eyes to see God's gifts all through your day.

As you look and search and find all the blessings God has given you, your heart will be full of praise.

Father, You have blessed me with every good thing. Help me to see them and praise You for them, amen.

TODAY WITH JESUS . . . READ PSALM 23 AND THANK HIM FOR ALL HE DOES.

PRAISE HIM

*Praise, glory, wisdom, thanks, honor, power, and
strength belong to our God forever and ever.*
REVELATION 7:12

There is nothing more wonderful than simply being with God and getting to know Him better. Of course, if you have no idea who God is, it will be hard for you to be still and praise Him. But when you understand who God really is—the Creator of you and all the universe—and what He's done for you, you won't be able to keep quiet about Him. You'll want to praise Him with all your heart.

So, right now, empty your mind of all your worries. Imagine that you are sitting right at the foot of His heavenly throne. Just think of how beautiful He is, how powerful, how wise, and how much He loves you. This is the God who invites you to come and sit with Him. How amazing is that! Thank Him, praise Him, sing to Him, and let Him give you a glimpse of heaven as you sit with Him.

*Lord, You are amazing, awesome, and worthy
of all my praise. I love You, amen.*

TODAY WITH JESUS . . . PRAISE HIS NAME.

GIVE THANKS ANYWAY

Always be joyful. . . . and give thanks whatever happens.
That is what God wants for you in Christ Jesus.
1 THESSALONIANS 5:16, 18 NCV

Sometimes being thankful is the last thing you want to do. Troubles, worries, sad times, hurtful people, and just plain bad days can steal your joy and take your thoughts away from God.

But if you ask God to make you thankful, He will! If you tell Him you really want to praise Him, but it's just hard right now, then He'll fill your mind with reminders of all His blessings. He will take your thoughts off your troubles and put them on Him and His many gifts to you.

Why does God do this? Because God commanded you to praise Him—and He wants to help you obey Him. Even in bad times, God wants you to see the good that comes from following Him (Romans 8:28). Ask God to make you thankful—and then praise Him when He does.

Lord, it's hard to be thankful some days. On those days,
please remind me of all Your blessings and gifts, amen.

TODAY WITH JESUS . . . BE THANKFUL.

THE PERFECT ATTITUDE

Be full of joy in the Lord always. I will say again, be full of joy.
PHILIPPIANS 4:4

Praising God is one of the most powerful things you can do as His child. That's because the Lord actually works through the praises of His people. When you tell God how much you love and appreciate Him, then you're admitting you need Him to take care of you and make you strong. And that's the perfect attitude for God to show His power through you.

Think about Paul and Silas. Even though they'd done nothing wrong, they were beaten, arrested, and thrown into a Philippian jail. But what did they do? They sang praises to God! And God worked through their praises by sending an earthquake to shake the prison doors open. The jailer was so amazed by the way God saved Paul and Silas that he and all his household became followers of Jesus.

So praise God—no matter what's happening in your life. And watch to see how He works through your praises.

*Jesus, I praise You! Even when I'm having a terrible day,
I know You're doing great things in my life, amen.*

TODAY WITH JESUS . . . SING A SONG OF PRAISE TO HIM.

POWER IN PRAISE

*I will be glad because of your love. You saw
my suffering. You knew my troubles.*

PSALM 31:7

As you get ready to start your day, you have a choice to make: you can grumble and complain about everything that's going wrong, *or* you can decide to praise God anyway.

But before you choose, remember this important truth: there's power in praise. Not only do you give God the thanks He deserves, but you also put your thoughts on Him and His blessings instead of yourself and your troubles—and that puts you on your way to a great day.

Of course, if you're facing a really big problem, it may be hard to praise God. So ask Him to help you. Pray, "Lord, I can't see all my blessings, because of this problem. But I know You're here and helping me." Believe God is in control and that He'll bring good out of everything you face. Choose to praise Him.

*Lord, I love You! You are wonderful and amazing
and worthy of all my praise, amen.*

TODAY WITH JESUS . . . CHOOSE TO PRAISE HIM.

THE GOOD STUFF

"Those who want to do right more than anything else are happy. God will fully satisfy them."
MATTHEW 5:6

Everyone wants the "good stuff" in life—good family, good friends, good fun. But here's the thing: God's idea of "good stuff" may be different from yours. You can try to get what you want your own way, but you'll probably end up disappointed. God's blessings, however, never let you down.

If you search for God every day then you'll find a joy that's much bigger than being popular, the latest and greatest game, or anything this world can offer you. And the more you learn about God, the more you'll want to get to know Him better. That's how Paul was able to say, "All things are worth nothing compared with the greatness of knowing Christ Jesus my Lord" (Philippians 3:8).

The very best blessings are those that bring you closer to Jesus and His plan for your life. So search for Him with all your heart—and He'll bless you with the really "good stuff."

Jesus, more than anything else, I want to get to know You better, amen.

TODAY WITH JESUS . . . BE HAPPY WITH GOD'S GOOD STUFF.

WITH LOVE AND GENTLENESS

*"God did not send his Son into the world to judge the
world guilty, but to save the world through him."*

JOHN 3:17

Have you ever messed up and then had to deal with everybody judging you for your mistake—even other Christians? Being judged is never fun, but when other Christians act like they've never made a mistake or sinned, it's downright painful.

When a child of God sins, God wants His other children to love them and gently guide them back to Him. But sadly, some people get so caught up in "punishing" the person who sinned—and in patting themselves on the back for being "better" than that person—that they actually end up chasing that person away from God!

If you know someone who's doing something wrong, don't punish him with your judgment. Instead, talk to him about God with love in your heart and gentleness in your words. Treat him the way you'd want to be treated. After all, everyone messes up and everyone sins—that's why Jesus came to offer forgiveness to everyone.

*Lord, help me treat others with the same love
and grace You give to me, amen.*

TODAY WITH JESUS . . . BE GENTLE WITH OTHERS.

DECEMBER

ALL CLUTTERED UP

"What is the seed that fell among the thorny weeds? That seed is like the person who hears the teaching but lets worries about this life and love of money stop that teaching from growing."
MATTHEW 13:22

Have you ever been listening to your teacher, but two minutes later you can't remember a thing she said? The same thing can happen in church or even when you're reading the Bible. That's because your mind can get cluttered up with other things. Things like worries—about yesterday's mistakes, today's troubles, or what might happen tomorrow. And when your mind is cluttered, it's hard to hear God.

Of course, it's okay to think about things—you need to do that. But the Devil wants stuff to get stuck in your thoughts, so that it's hard to hear God. Defeat the Devil by telling God your worries, and trusting Him to take care of them. Then turn to the Psalms and start to read. Let the verses help you praise God for who He is and what He's done. As your mind clears and you focus on Him, you'll soon feel His peace and hear His voice.

Father, I give all my worries to You. I know You'll take care of everything I need, amen.

TODAY WITH JESUS . . . READ PSALM 19:1 AND THINK ABOUT WHO GOD IS.

ALL TO HIMSELF

*Early the next morning, Jesus woke and left the house while
it was still dark. He went to a place to be alone and pray.*

MARK 1:35

If Jesus, the holy Son of God, needed to go off by Himself to pray, don't you think you should too?

God wants you to be alone with Him. Why? Because He wants your full attention—free from the distractions of TV, other people, or just plain noise. Because it's in the quiet time, when you're alone with Him, that you can share everything in your heart—your joys, sorrows, worries, and fears.

God wants you all to Himself so He can wrap you up in His loving arms and remind you of all His promises. But if you aren't willing to make time to be alone with Him, you won't experience this blessing. Your mind will be pulled in too many different directions. Don't let anything keep you away from your time alone with God—it's one of your most precious gifts.

*Father, thank You for wanting to be alone with
me. I love You with all my heart, amen.*

TODAY WITH JESUS . . . BE ALONE WITH HIM.

DECEMBER 3

GIVE EVERYTHING TO HIM

Don't you realize that you become the slave
of whatever you choose to obey?
ROMANS 6:16 NLT

Have you ever had a favorite shirt? You loved that shirt, but you outgrew it. There was nothing wrong with it. It just wasn't a good fit anymore. And it was taking up space that could be better used for clothes that did fit. So your parents asked you to give it up.

Sometimes God does the same thing. He may ask you to give up something—like a hobby, a sport, or even a friendship. Not because it's sinful, but because it's pulling you away from Him. It just doesn't fit His plan for your life anymore. And it's taking up space that would be better used for Him.

Are you willing to give up everything for God? Not just sinful things, but good things too? Ask God to help you say, "Everything I have is Yours, Lord." Because no matter what God asks you to give up, He'll bless you with something even better.

Lord, help me be willing to give up anything You ask
me to—I want to be completely Yours, amen.

TODAY WITH JESUS . . . BE READY TO
GIVE EVERYTHING TO HIM.

ONE OF GOD'S GREATEST TOOLS

I am happy when I have weaknesses, insults, hard times, sufferings, and all kinds of troubles. All these things are for Christ. And I am happy, because when I am weak, then I am truly strong.

2 CORINTHIANS 12:10

Extreme pressure can transform a lump of coal into a beautiful diamond. In the same way, the pressures of tough times and troubles can transform you into a shining light for God's kingdom. That's because God works through the hard times and troubles in your life. He uses them to transform your heart, change your way of thinking, teach you to trust Him, and help you walk closer to Him.

You see, troubles are actually one of God's greatest tools. He uses them to build you into the person He created you to be, to pull you closer to Jesus, and to train you to serve Him.

God has a purpose for every trouble and every tough time that He allows to come into your life. So don't be discouraged when you face problems. Instead, ask God to show you what He is trying to teach you—and then learn from Him.

Lord, I trust You to use every trouble that comes into my life for my own good, amen.

THE FATHER KNOWS BEST

God knows that if you eat the fruit from that tree, you will learn about good and evil. Then you will be like God!
GENESIS 3:5

Satan tricked Eve . . . in a very sneaky way. First he tempted her pride by saying, "Eve, you're going to be like God. You're going to know good and evil." But what Satan *didn't* tell her is that Eve would hate the day she learned about sin and death.

Be warned: anyone can fall for one of Satan's tricks. He likes to trick you into disobeying God by telling you only part of the story—just like he did with Eve. What he doesn't bother to tell you is what happens *after* you disobey God because it is always bad. Don't fall for his tricks.

Satan used Eve's own pride to trick her. And he'll try to do the same thing to you. Because every time you choose to disobey God, what you're really saying is, "God, I know better than you." That's pride. And that's also very, very foolish.

Your heavenly Father always knows best—listen to Him.

Father, it's so easy to start thinking I know better than You do. Forgive me, and help me trust that You really know what's best, amen.

TODAY WITH JESUS . . . REMEMBER HE ALWAYS KNOWS AND PROVIDES WHAT IS BEST FOR YOU.

YOU CAN'T CHANGE YOURSELF

*I do not live anymore—it is Christ living in me. I still
live in my body, but I live by faith in the Son of God.
He loved me and gave himself to save me.*

GALATIANS 2:20

You know what you should do—read God's Word and think about it every day, believe His promises, and trust Him to take care of you when times get tough. So you make a plan. You'll read the Bible at this time, pray at that time, and you'll trust Him no matter what. But then you don't stick to the plan, so you make another one . . . and another one. But your plans never quite work out.

Perhaps your real problem is that you trust Jesus to save you, but you don't really trust Him to change your life. So you try to do it yourself—which, of course, doesn't work. That's because you can't change yourself, but God can! When you decide to follow Jesus, the Holy Spirit of God comes to live inside you. It's His job to change you—and it's your job to let Him.

*Lord, only You can really change me. Make
me more and more like You, amen.*

**TODAY WITH JESUS . . . ASK THE HOLY SPIRIT
CHANGE YOU—AND THEN LET HIM.**

HEART CHECK

"Don't let your hearts be troubled. Trust in God. And trust in me."
JOHN 14:1

There's something you probably do almost every day, and you don't even know it. What is it? *Give up your peace.*

You take your focus off God and let the sins of this world creep into your life. It could be things you know are wrong, or it could be things you might not even think of as sin, like having a bad attitude, angry thoughts, or just doing things your own way instead of trusting God to lead you.

But there's a way to hold on to your peace: do a "heart check" every day. Talk to God and ask Him to show you any sin that's crept into your life. Ask Him to forgive you and help you get back on the right track.

Start your day today with a "heart check." Because when you give your day to Him, He gives His peace to you.

Holy Father, look into my heart and show
me what I need to change, amen.

TODAY WITH JESUS . . . ASK GOD
TO CHECK YOUR HEART.

OKAY TO SAY NO?

So be careful how you live. Don't live like fools, but like those who are wise. Make the most of every opportunity.

EPHESIANS 5:15–16 NLT

Are you afraid to say no? Do you worry what people will think if you do? Of course, you should say no to bad things, like drugs and alcohol and candy from strangers. But what about "good" things—can you say no to them?

Yes, you can! There are so many good things—friend things, family things, church things, and even helping things. But if you say yes to every good thing, then you won't have time for the very best: God. And even though you're doing good things—maybe even good things for God—you'll miss out on the peace and joy He promised you.

That's why it's important to say no sometimes, so that you can say yes to God. Remember, Jesus took time away from the good things of His ministry to be alone with His Father. If Jesus needed to do that, how much more do you?

God, please show me the things I should say yes to and the things I should say no to, amen.

TODAY WITH JESUS . . . SAY YES TO TIME WITH HIM.

HOW GOD SEES TROUBLES

We have small troubles for a while now, but they are helping us gain an eternal glory. That glory is much greater than the troubles.
2 CORINTHIANS 4:17

When troubles and tough times come into your life, it's easy to think only about them and how they're messing up your life. But don't forget about God—and the fact that He sees these troubles in a completely different way. For Him, your difficulties are tools. God uses your struggles to shape and change you. They become part of His perfect plan to give you His character and give you purpose.

Are there any "small troubles" or not-so-small troubles in your life today? If so, ask God to help you see them through His eyes. Because then you'll see that those troubles are actually part of His plan to bless you more than you could ever imagine.

So when problems start pulling you down, ask God to carry them for you—it's what He wants to do. And then trust Him to not only help you, but also bless you through them.

Father, it's so easy to see only the problems. Please also show me how You're using them to bless me, amen.

TODAY WITH JESUS . . . TRUST HIM TO TURN TROUBLES INTO BLESSINGS.

LOVE THE UNLOVABLE

If someone says, "I love God," but hates his brother, he
is a liar. He can see his brother, but he hates him. So
he cannot love God, whom he has never seen.

1 JOHN 4:20

It's a sad fact of life: there will always be someone who gets on your nerves. There will always be someone who knows just how to "push your buttons" and make you angry, annoyed, or even afraid. It would be so easy to hate that person and, maybe, to try to get even with him. But look at today's verse—that's not what God wants you to do.

That person is *not* your enemy. Instead, God has allowed that person to come into your life to teach you things like patience, kindness, and forgiveness. That person doesn't need your revenge—he needs your grace.

Show God you trust Him by asking Him to give you the strength to be patient, to forgive, and to love that person just as He does. It may not be what you want to do, but remember: patience, kindness, forgiveness, and grace are exactly what God gives to you.

Father, please give me the strength to love and
forgive others as You love and forgive me,-amen.

TODAY WITH JESUS . . . LOVE THE UNLOVABLE.

TURN TO HIM

We live by what we believe, not by what we can see.
2 CORINTHIANS 5:7

There's a reason for everything that happens in your life today—even the problems. Yes, some problems may be because of a bad choice. But some are troubles God has allowed into your life to teach you and make your faith in Him even stronger (1 Peter 1:6–7). You see, God knows *everything*, and He knows just what you need to teach you to count on Him instead of your own way of doing things.

But you may be thinking, *I have no idea what to do about this problem. I need help now!* And that's exactly what God wants. Because it is usually when you have no idea about what to do that you turn to Him. God wants to show you that He's all-powerful and able to handle whatever you face. Turn to Him, tell Him everything, and trust Him to help you. Then watch as He shows you who He really is.

*Lord, You are all-powerful and all-knowing. Help
me trust You to take care of me, amen.*

**TODAY WITH JESUS . . . TURN TO
HIM WITH YOUR TROUBLES.**

THINK ABOUT HIM

*I look at the heavens, which you made with your hands. I
see the moon and stars, which you created. But why is man
important to you? Why do you take care of human beings?*

PSALM 8:3–4

Today, take some time to think about God. There is no end to His power, His creativity, or His love for you. Consider how He created the whole universe—planning the paths of the stars, the planets, and the galaxies—and even giving each of them a name! That same God knows you, and He wants you to get to know Him.

Nothing is impossible for God. At His command, the earth was formed (Genesis 1), the Red Sea parted (Exodus 14), and the sun and moon stood still in the sky (Joshua 10:13). He even sacrificed His own Son so that your enemies of sin and death could be defeated forever (1 Corinthians 15:54–57).

And He loves *you*!

Today, remember that God is right by your side. Turn to Him for everything you face. Because He is your protector and your Lord, there's nothing for you to be afraid of.

*Lord God, nothing is impossible for You! I praise
You and thank You for loving me, amen.*

TODAY WITH JESUS . . . THINK ABOUT ALL HE CREATED.

BELIEVE HE FORGIVES

When our hearts make us feel guilty, we can still have peace before
God. God is greater than our hearts, and he knows everything.
1 JOHN 3:20

Have you ever said, "I know God has forgiven me, but I just can't forgive myself"? You did something you knew was wrong, you asked God to forgive you, and you know He did—but you just can't seem to stop feeling guilty. How can you get rid of those feelings?

- *Admit*: First, admit that you haven't forgiven yourself.
- *Tell*: Tell God that you know not forgiving yourself is also a sin—the sin of not trusting His promise to make you fully clean. Then accept His forgiveness completely.
- *Believe God*: Believe He really has taken away your sins—"as far as the east is from the west" (Psalm 103:12).
- *Choose*: Because Jesus died for you on the cross, choose to forgive yourself.

Dear child of God, He has promised to forgive you. Believe His promise and let go of the guilt and shame.

> *Lord, thank You for forgiving me. Help me to*
> *trust Your grace and forgive myself, amen.*

TODAY WITH JESUS . . . BELIEVE HE FORGIVES YOU.

A LIGHT FOR YOUR LIFE

Your word is like a lamp for my feet and a light for my way.
PSALM 119:105

The Bible is a light for your life. It chases away the Devil's darkness. But when you don't read from God's Word every day, it's much easier for the Devil to attack. And one of his favorite ways to attack is by lying about God's Word. But if you know what the Bible really says, you can spot his lies.

Remember, Satan will do anything to turn you away from God. He'll tempt you, discourage you, and lie to you. He'll especially lie about God's promises. For example, God's Word says that if you confess and repent of your sin, God will forgive you (1 John 1:9). But Satan will lie and say your sin is too terrible to forgive. Then he'll try to keep you away from God by making you feel ashamed and guilty. That's why it's important to shine the light of God's truth on the Devil's lies—so read His Word every day!

Father, thank You for the light and
protection of Your Word, amen.

TODAY WITH JESUS . . . READ ABOUT GOD'S
ARMOR IN EPHESIANS 6:10–18.

FACING THE STORMS

We have sufferings now. But the sufferings we have now are
nothing compared to the great glory that will be given to us.
ROMANS 8:18

Many of your greatest victories with God will come from the storms you face—*if* you face them together with Him.

For example, when Jesus' disciples were out on the Sea of Galilee, they faced a storm so terrible they thought they were going to die. But Jesus spoke just a few words to the storm, and instantly the waves stopped crashing and the wind was silent. The disciples never forgot that. So when they faced other storms—prison, beatings, and persecution—they wouldn't stop teaching about Jesus. Why? Because they knew He was more powerful than any kind of storm (Acts 5:40–42). And many people followed Jesus because of them.

If you're facing a storm that's just too big for you to handle, turn to Jesus. Give your fear, hurt, worry, and sadness to Him. Let Him still your storm—and then let Him use you to tell others about Him.

Jesus, there are times when I'm worried and afraid, but
I'll trust You to see me safely through any storm, amen.

TODAY WITH JESUS . . . TRUST HIM IN EVERY STORM.

STAY AWAY FROM SIN

Everyone who believes is free from all sins through him.

ACTS 13:39

Sin isn't just a problem—it's a *big* problem. It will sneak into your life, mess up the way you think, and tempt you to make bad choices. God knew you could never beat sin on your own, so He sent Jesus to defeat it for you.

However . . . just because you follow Jesus, that doesn't mean you'll never sin again. But if you stay close to Jesus every day, He'll help you not to sin. First, you must be honest with Jesus. Tell Him the sins you struggle with and ask Him to help you beat them. Agree with Him that your sins really are wrong—don't make excuses or pretend they're okay. And then ask Him to show you how to think and live in a way that pleases Him.

Stay close to Jesus—by praying, reading His Word, and obeying Him—and He'll help you stay away from sin.

Lord Jesus, help me turn to You and
turn away from my sin, amen.

TODAY WITH JESUS . . . STAY CLOSE TO HIM.

SURPRISE!

Why am I so sad? Why am I so upset? I should put
my hope in God. I should keep praising him.
PSALM 42:5

Surprise! Wow, you did *not* see that coming—and now your feelings are about to explode out of you. If the surprise is good, and the feelings are joy and happiness, then you may be a little shaken up, but you're still okay. But if the surprise is bad, and the feelings are anger, pain, or sadness, then the hurt can go deep and last a long time.

When you get a bad surprise—whether it's terrible news, a friend's betrayal, or hurtful words—you have a choice to make. You can just let those feelings explode out of you. *Or* you can run to God, because that bad surprise doesn't have to be a bad thing, if you let it pull you closer to Him.

So get down on your knees, open up the Bible, and ask God to show you what you should do—and what He can teach you through this. Then let Him hold you close and comfort your heart.

Lord, help me turn to You every day, but especially
when bad things catch me by surprise, amen.

TODAY WITH JESUS . . . ASK HIM TO HELP
YOU CONTROL YOUR FEELINGS.

BELIEVE THE TRUTH

"You will know the truth. And the truth will make you free."

JOHN 8:32

The Devil likes to lie. And one of his favorite lies is that you're not good enough—you're not worthy, you're not able, and nobody loves you. He knows that if he can push you down and get you to believe his lies, then you won't experience the power, love, and freedom that God created you to enjoy. Don't listen to the Devil.

Instead, listen to this truth: you are a child of God—created by Him with love, bought with the blood of Jesus, and home to the Holy Spirit who lives inside you. You are endlessly loved, able to do whatever He asks of you, and so very precious to Him.

That's the truth—and the Bible says it over and over again. Whenever you start to doubt it, that's when you're listening to one of the Devil's lies. Believe in who God says you are—His opinion is the only one that matters.

*Father, show me the Devil's lies and teach
me who I really am, amen.*

**TODAY WITH JESUS . . . READ THE BIBLE
AND DISCOVER WHO YOU REALLY ARE.**

LOVE YOUR ENEMIES

"Love your enemies. Do good to those who hate you."
LUKE 6:27

Have you ever felt like you were fighting a battle, and then someone you knew made it even harder to fight? Not only did that person not help you, but he or she seemed to be fighting against you. For example, maybe you were getting picked on by someone at school. And then, instead of sticking up for you, a person you thought was your friend started saying mean things too! What do you do with those kinds of people?

Jesus knew you would have those kinds of enemies in your life. And He asks you to love them. Why? Because *He* loves them.

You can't change your enemies, but you can control how you treat them (Luke 23:34). And Jesus asks you to treat them with love so they can learn about Him through you. Pray for them and do good things for them, because then you show them who Jesus is.

Lord, help me show Your love to all people—even my enemies—so they will learn about You, amen.

TODAY WITH JESUS . . . DO GOOD TO YOUR ENEMIES.

TRUST AND OBEY

Mary said, "I am the servant girl of the Lord.
Let this happen to me as you say!"

LUKE 1:38

If Jesus asks you to do something and you do it, then you can be sure He'll bless you. And that blessing will often be shared by those around you.

Think about Mary. The angel Gabriel came to her and said, "Listen! You will become pregnant. You will give birth to a son, and you will name him Jesus" (Luke 1:31). Mary was just a young girl. She knew that people wouldn't understand or believe what God had called her to do—have a baby while she was still an unmarried virgin. But she obeyed God anyway—and because she did, the whole world was blessed with a Savior.

Mary knew that obeying God would not be an easy thing, but she still said yes. She didn't question God's plans or try to figure out a different way. She simply trusted and obeyed Him. And that's what God wants you to do, too. Don't doubt, don't try to figure out an easier way. Simply trust and obey whatever He tells you to do.

Lord, help me trust You enough to obey
even when it's not easy, amen.

TODAY WITH JESUS . . . BE WILLING TO OBEY.

DECEMBER 21

LIGHT OF YOUR WORLD

"For you who honor me, goodness will shine on you
like the sun. There will be healing in its rays."
MALACHI 4:2

Christmas is a wonderful time to remember why Jesus came. Your Savior came to shine His light into the darkness of your sins—to forgive you, heal you, and make you whole again. Jesus doesn't use His light just to point out your sins. He also uses it to uncover the fears, pain, and wrong ways of thinking that cause you to sin in the first place.

How does Jesus do this? Through His Word. When you read the Bible and ask the Holy Spirit to show you what it means, He'll show you the things that are pulling you away from Him and causing you to sin (Hebrews 4:12)—things like someone you haven't forgiven, a bad attitude, or a quick temper.

This Christmas, invite Jesus to shine His light into your heart and mind. Ask Him what you need to change—and thank Him for the wonderful gift of His love and light.

Jesus, shine Your light of truth into my heart and my
mind. Show me what I need to change, amen.

**TODAY WITH JESUS . . . LET HIS
LIGHT SHINE IN YOUR LIFE.**

JESUS, YOUR HIGH PRIEST

For our high priest is able to understand our weaknesses. He was tempted in every way that we are, but he did not sin.

HEBREWS 4:15

When you have a problem, it can be hard to know who to go to for help. Who will really understand? Who will know what to do? And who will be willing to help?

In the Old Testament people went to the priests for help. The priests spoke for God and tried to help others understand Him. But they were only human, and sometimes they made mistakes.

But when Jesus came, He became a high priest unlike any other. Jesus doesn't just speak for God—*He is God*. He is all-knowing, so He understands you perfectly, and He knows exactly how to help you. He is all-powerful, so He's able to give you exactly what you need. And He is endlessly loving, so He's always willing to help.

Whether or not you have a problem, go to Jesus. You'll find Him—and you'll also find His wisdom, mercy, power, and love.

Jesus, thank You for being the One I can always go to, amen.

TODAY WITH JESUS . . . GO TO HIM.

A BETTER PLAN

When the right time came, God sent his Son.
GALATIANS 4:4

What are you waiting for this Christmas? Is it the Christmas candy, a party, or a present? There are so many good things to wait and hope for in the Christmas season, but the very best one has already come: your Savior.

But Jesus didn't come when or how the world was expecting Him to. The people of Israel thought their Savior would come as a conqueror to set them free from their enemies. But He didn't. They also thought He would come as a great and mighty king to rule over the kingdom of Israel on earth. Instead, He came as a helpless baby in a manger.

Israel had a plan for their Savior, but God had a better one. He didn't send His Son to save a nation; He sent Jesus to save souls. Remember, you may have a plan, but trust God and follow Him—because He has a better one.

> *Lord, I will trust Your ways and Your plans—*
> *they're always better than mine, amen.*

TODAY WITH JESUS . . . TRUST HIS PLAN.

YOUR PRINCE OF PEACE

*Give glory to God in heaven, and on earth let there
be peace to the people who please God.*

LUKE 2:14

Christmas is a busy time with all its plays and parties and presents. But it can also be a stressful time—because of all the things you need to do and places you need to be. The angels who came to tell about Jesus' birth promised peace to His people, but right now you may be feeling anything but peace.

When all the hustle and bustle of Christmas has you feeling worn out and overwhelmed, stop and take a deep breath. Then remember this truth: Jesus wants to give you peace—and He is able to do it, even in the middle of this busy season (John 14:27).

When your days seem to be spinning out of control, remember that Jesus has everything under His control (Psalm 103:19). Trust Him to give you the peace you need as you obey Him. Remember that He'll never leave you or let you down. And He's always ready, willing, and able to help (Psalm 46:1).

*Jesus, thank You for being my Prince of
Peace. You give me joy forever, amen.*

TODAY WITH JESUS . . . LET HIM GIVE YOU PEACE.

DECEMBER 25

HIS GIFT

"They will name him Immanuel. This name means 'God is with us.'"
MATTHEW 1:23

This Christmas Day, think about this amazing truth: the Lord—the ruler and Creator of everything—became a man and walked in the dust of this earth so that He could know what it's like to be you (Hebrews 2:17).

"He gave up his place with God and made himself nothing. He was born as a man and became like a servant. . . . He humbled himself and was fully obedient to God. He obeyed even when that caused his death—death on a cross" (Philippians 2:7–8). That's how much Jesus loves you. And if that wasn't enough, He sent His own Holy Spirit to live inside you—to guide you and comfort you.

You have been given the most amazing gift imaginable—a Savior who loves you, understands you, and helps you always. You are never alone and never helpless. God Himself is always with you. Praise Him for His indescribable gift!

Jesus, thank You for the amazing gift of Your Holy Spirit, amen.

TODAY WITH JESUS . . . THANK HIM FOR HIS GIFT.

THE BLESSING OF FRIENDS

A man who has friends must himself be friendly.

PROVERBS 18:24 NKJV

The Lord wants to be your very best friend, but that's not all He wants for you. He also wants you to have strong and wonderful friendships with the people around you. When you are lonely, you should go to God first. But after that, you should also turn to the people He has put in your life.

One of the greatest blessings in life is a friend who loves God and who helps you love Him even more. When you're feeling lonely or upset or ready to give up, go to your friends. That's why God has put them in your life—to love you, to spend time with you, to laugh together, to have fun together, and also to help each other.

God never meant for you to live your life on your own. Reach out to others, make friends—and then thank God for your friendships.

Father, please put friends in my life who love You and will help me love You more. And help me be that same kind of friend to them, amen.

TODAY WITH JESUS . . . LOOK FOR FRIENDS WHO LOVE GOD.

NO WORRIES

"None of you can add any time to your life by worrying about it."
LUKE 12:25

Do you worry about the future? As this new year is about to begin, are you concerned about what will happen? Do you worry if you'll fit in at school or about your parents' jobs, your health, or your grades?

Worry can make you feel stressed and hopeless and worn out—but it doesn't actually do *anything* to help you! So instead of fretting, talk to Jesus. He's the only One who can protect you from your troubles and fill your mind with peace.

As you talk to Him, you'll see that He understands your fears—because Jesus was human once, just like you. He'll pull you close to Him and help you with whatever you're scared about. He won't leave you alone for a second. There still may be troubles and hard times to face—but as long as you stay close to Him, He'll take care of you and everything that worries you.

*Jesus, please take away my worries and
fears. Help me to trust You, amen.*

**TODAY WITH JESUS . . . THINK ABOUT
HIM, NOT YOUR WORRIES.**

ALWAYS WELCOME

Let us, then, feel free to come before God's throne. Here there is grace.
And we can receive mercy and grace to help us when we need it.

HEBREWS 4:16

Because you're a child, there are some places you just aren't welcome—like the teachers' break room, your mom's business meeting, or maybe even your dad's garage. But as *a child of God*, there's one place you're *always* welcome—with God.

Even if you've sinned, God wants you to come to Him. Confess your sins, and He'll forgive you completely. There's no need to feel any shame. But watch out for the Devil. He likes to trick you into feeling ashamed, so that you'll try to hide from God like Adam and Eve did (Genesis 3:10). And the more the Devil can get you to focus on your shame, the easier it is for him to keep you away from the Father, who is always willing to forgive you.

God wants you with Him, no matter what you've done or how you feel (Psalm 34:18). Go to Him! He's just waiting to wrap you up in His loving—and forgiving—arms.

Lord, thank You for forgiving my sins. I'm so
grateful that I can always come to You, amen.

TODAY WITH JESUS . . . YOU ARE
ALWAYS WELCOME WITH HIM.

WHEN THE ODDS ARE AGAINST YOU

"Get up! The Lord has defeated the army of Midian for you!"
JUDGES 7:15

Gideon faced the biggest challenge of his entire life. He had to fight a huge army of Midianites with only three hundred men. But God was on his side, and He helped Gideon in an amazing way.

As Gideon spied on the enemy's camp, he was more than a little frightened. But then he heard two of his enemies talking about a dream. The dream meant that God was going to let Gideon's army win, so the two men were terrified. But Gideon was thrilled, and he praised God. His fear was replaced with boldness because he realized God had already defeated his enemies—now he just had to wait and watch it happen.

When the odds seem to be against you, remember that God hasn't left you to face your enemies alone. He already has a plan to rescue you—so praise Him and let Him replace your fears with boldness.

Lord, I will trust You even when everything looks hopeless. I know You'll rescue me, amen.

TODAY WITH JESUS . . . BE BOLD.

EXPECT HIM TO HELP

You will teach me God's way to live. Being with you will fill me
with joy. At your right hand I will find pleasure forever.

PSALM 16:11

A new year is almost here. Are there things you're looking forward to? Or things you're dreading? Maybe there's something you think God is asking you to do, but you don't see how you can do it. Perhaps it's to help someone in need, serve at your church, or talk to *that* person—the one who's just plain mean to you—about Jesus.

Remember this: you may not see how you can do what God asks you to do, but God does. And He'll give you everything you need to succeed as you obey Him.

So what should you do while you're waiting for Him to provide you with what you need? Remember all the ways He's helped you in the past. Ask Him to guide you, and spend time in His Word. And then, praise Him for the help you know is coming.

Lord, sometimes the things You ask me to do seem
impossible, but I'll trust You to make them possible, amen.

TODAY WITH JESUS . . . EXPECT HIM TO HELP YOU.

DECEMBER 31

ALWAYS KING

On his robe and on his leg was written this name:
"KING OF KINGS AND LORD OF LORDS."
REVELATION 19:16

Today is the last day of this year. As you look back over the past year, how has your life changed? What blessings have come into your life? What problems have you faced and overcome? What has surprised you? Even though you're young, you're probably finding out that life is full of changes.

But if you only think about how your life is always changing, it can make you feel uncertain and worried about your future. Let this truth give you courage and hope for your future: *your God never changes.* He's always faithful, always with you, always loves you, and always in control. There's no challenge He can't help you through and no problem too big for Him to solve.

As this new year begins, take joy in knowing that the One who is always King is also the One who is always with you. And that fact will never change.

Lord, thank You for always being with me. Help me
to get to know You better in this new year, amen.

TODAY WITH JESUS . . . DECIDE TO
GET TO KNOW HIM BETTER.

ABOUT THE AUTHOR

Dr. Charles Stanley is the senior pastor of the First Baptist Church of Atlanta, where he has served for more than 40 years. He is a *New York Times* bestselling author who has written more than 60 books, including the bestselling devotional *Every Day in His Presence*. Dr. Stanley is the founder of In Touch Ministries. The *In Touch with Dr. Charles Stanley* program is transmitted throughout the world on more than 1,200 radio outlets and 130 television stations/networks, and in language projects in more than 50 languages. The award-winning *In Touch* devotional magazine is printed in four languages with more than 12 million copies each year. Dr. Stanley's goal is best represented by Acts 20:24: "Life is worth nothing unless I use it for doing the work assigned me by the Lord Jesus—the work of telling others the Good News about God's mighty kindness and love." This is because, as he says, "It is the Word of God and the work of God that changes people's lives."